Karen Brown's
FRANCE

Charming Bed & Breakfasts

Written by

KAREN BROWN and CLARE BROWN

Illustrations by Barbara Tapp
Cover Painting by Jann Pollard

Karen Brown's Guides, San Mateo, California

Karen Brown Titles

Austria: Charming Inns & Itineraries

California: Charming Inns & Itineraries

England: Charming Bed & Breakfasts

England, Wales & Scotland: Charming Hotels & Itineraries

France: Charming Bed & Breakfasts

France: Charming Inns & Itineraries

Germany: Charming Inns & Itineraries

Ireland: Charming Inns & Itineraries

Italy: Charming Bed & Breakfasts

Italy: Charming Inns & Itineraries

Portugal: Charming Inns & Itineraries

Spain: Charming Inns & Itineraries

Switzerland: Charming Inns & Itineraries

Dedicated with boundless love
to
Heidi and Bill
Karen and Rick
Kim and Christian

Editors: Karen Brown, June Brown, Clare Brown, Kim Brown Holmsen, Iris Sandilands, Lorena Aburto.

Illustrations: Barbara Tapp; Cover painting: Jann Pollard; Webmistress: Lynn Upthagrove.

Maps: Susanne Lau Alloway—Greenleaf Design & Graphics; Inside cover photo: W. Russell Ohlson.

Distributed by Fodor's Travel Publications, Inc., 201 East 50th Street, New York, NY 10022, USA.

Distributed in Canada by Random House Canada, 2775 Matheson Boulevard. East, Mississanga, Ontario, Canada L4W4P7, phone (905) 624 0672, fax (905) 624 6217

Distributed in the United Kingdom, Ireland and Europe by Random House UK, 20 Vauxhall Bridge Road, London, SW1V 2SA, phone: 44 20 7840 4000, fax: 44 20 7840 8406.

Distributed in Australia by Random House Australia, 20 Alfred Street, Milsons Point, Sydney NSW 2061, Australia, phone: 61 2 9954 9966, fax: 61 2 9954 4562.

Distributed in New Zealand by Random House New Zealand, 18 Poland Road, Glenfield, Auckland, New Zealand, phone: 64 9 444 7197, fax: 64 9 444 7524.

Distributed in South Africa by Random House South Africa, Endulani, East Wing, 5A Jubilee Road, Parktown 2193, South Africa, phone: 27 11 484 3538, fax: 27 11 484 6180.

A catalog record for this book is available from the British Library.

Library of Congress Cataloging-in-Publication Data

Brown, Clare.
  Karen Brown's France : charming bed & breakfasts / written by
Clare Brown ; illustrations by Barbara Tapp ;   cover painting by Jann
Pollard.
    p.   cm. -- (Karen Brown's country inn series)
  Includes index.
  ISBN 0-930328-88-4
  1.   Bed and breakfast accommodations--France Guidebooks. 2. France
Guidebooks.   I. Brown, Karen, 1956- . II. Title.   III. Series.
  TX907.5.F7B75 2000
  647.9444'03--DC21   99-15256
                                                                   CIP

The painting on the front cover is of the town of Vezelay

Contents

Introduction

Travelers with a sense of adventure can truly experience France and get to know the French people by journeying beyond Paris and exploring the countryside. The way of life outside Paris ("in the provinces," as the French say) is a fascinating reflection of French history and culture—the impact of modern civilization is felt, but a pronounced respect for tradition and quality of life remains. Beyond Paris, the land is like a treasure chest: royal forests with graceful deer, romantic castles casting their images onto serene lakes, picturesque villages with half-timbered houses, vineyards edged with roses, meadows of fragrant lavender, fields of vibrant yellow sunflowers, medieval walled cities perched upon mountain tops, and wild coastlines—all waiting to be discovered.

ABOUT BED & BREAKFAST TRAVEL

The bed and breakfast formula is for any traveler who wants to experience the **real** France, its people and culture. There is a social aspect to this style of travel that is not found in the normal tourist experience. You have ample opportunities to meet and exchange ideas with other travelers (usually Europeans) as well as to get to know your hosts and their families, many times making lasting friendships. Single travelers will love the friendliness of bed and breakfast stays because they will not feel alone. Bed and breakfast travel is also tailor-made for families with children—the informality, convenience, and reasonable rates make travel a pleasure. *Note:* Many places also offer family accommodation with several bedrooms and a small kitchen.

ACCOMMODATIONS—WHAT TO EXPECT

Bed and breakfast accommodation, in most cases, means a bedroom rented in the private home of a French family. Throughout this guide, the French term *chez* used before a family name translates as "at the home of" and is an accurate phrase when describing the type of accommodation and ambiance that you can expect. However, do not feel that to travel the bed and breakfast route means you will be roughing it. Although some of the least expensive choices in our guide offer very simple rooms, it is possible to choose places to stay that offer sumptuous accommodations—as beautiful as you will find in the most luxurious hotels, at a fraction of the cost. So, this book is definitely not just for the budget-conscious traveler, but for anyone who wants to meet the French people and experience their exceptional hospitality.

The dividing line between a bed and breakfast and a "regular" hotel is sometimes very obscure. In essence, hotels are larger and offer more commercial amenities than a bed and breakfast—hotels usually have a reception desk, a staff member always on the premises, a public restaurant, telephones in the rooms, and a porter for luggage. However, nothing is truly black and white. Some of the bed and breakfasts featured in this guide are very sophisticated and offer every imaginable nicety including exquisite linens, fluffy bathrobes, towel warmers, hairdryers, and an assortment of the finest toiletries. As a rule of thumb, you will find that the bed and breakfast accommodations are far less expensive than a comparable room in a hotel, offer a more personalized warmth of welcome, and provide a better opportunity to meet other guests. *Note:* We have intentionally included a few simple, well-priced, small hotels with charm that are located in areas where we could not find a suitable bed and breakfast to offer you.

Hosts cover the entire spectrum of French society, from titled counts and countesses to country farmers. All who are listed in this guide are hospitable and have a true desire to meet and interact with their guests. It takes a special kind of person to open his home to strangers, and the French who do so are genuinely warm and friendly.

Bed and breakfasts are called *chambres d'hôtes* (literally, "guest bedrooms") and are most frequently situated in rural settings. This guide offers lodging selections in or near major tourist sites as well as in unspoiled, less-visited regions. Most hosts prefer that their bed and breakfast guests take the time to unwind by staying at least three nights (Americans have a reputation for always being in a hurry). Frequently discounts are offered for stays of a week or longer, but the advantages of longer stays in one place are far greater than just financial: it is great fun to become friends with the owners and other guests, to just *settle in*—no packing and unpacking every night. Frequently a house-party atmosphere prevails as you gather with other guests in the evening to share your travel adventures. We strongly urge you to choose one place to stay and make it your hub, going off in a different direction each day to explore the countryside. Spend time in a medieval stone-walled château evoking dreams of knights and their ladies or experience the sights and sounds of a simple farm surrounded by bucolic pasture lands. Careful reading of the descriptions in this guide will assure that the homes you select are consonant with the type of welcome and accommodation you prefer. Each home is, of course, unique, offering its own special charm, yet all share one wonderful common denominator: the welcoming feeling of being treated as a cherished guest in a friend's home. We unequivocally feel there is no finer way to travel in France.

We personally visited hundreds of bed and breakfasts, traveling to remote villages and hamlets throughout France to find the finest places to stay. Even after honing down our list by prior research, we usually included only about one out of every three places seen. We made our personal selection based on individual charm, antique ambiance, romantic feel, and above all, on warmth of welcome. We chose each place to stay on its merit alone. We selected in each region the most outstanding accommodations in various price ranges. Our choices are very subjective: we have hand-picked for you those places that we like the most and think you will also enjoy.

CAR RENTAL

Readers frequently ask our advice on car rental companies. We always use Auto Europe, a car rental broker that negotiates with the major car rental companies to obtain the lowest possible price. They also offer motor homes and chauffeur services. Auto Europe's toll-free phone service from every European country connects you to their US-based, 24-hour reservation center (ask for the card with European phone numbers to be sent to you). Auto Europe offers our readers a minimum of a 5% discount, and occasionally free upgrades. Karen Brown readers can also obtain a free car phone with rentals of 7 days or more. You will be responsible for the activation fee ($30), cost to ship the phone to your home ($30), and charge for time used. Be sure to use the Karen Brown ID number 99006187 to receive your discount and any special offers. You can make your own reservations via our website, www.karenbrown.com (select Auto Europe from the home page under Travel Center), or by phone (1-800-223-5555).

CHAMBRES D'HÔTES & GÎTES DE FRANCE

Over 5,600 bed and breakfasts in France belong to a national organization, Gîtes de France. Members of this organization usually display the green-and-yellow Gîtes de France logo shown. Chambres d'hôtes that are members of Gîtes de France have passed an in-depth inspection by the organization and conform to a high standard of welcome and comfort. We have worked very closely with this organization to select the finest

places to stay from an overwhelming list of possibilities. The majority of chambres d'hôtes featured in this guide are part of this association. However, we also visited and have included many outstanding places that have chosen not to belong to the Gîtes de France. In the bed and breakfast description section we have put "Gîtes de France" by the name of all the properties that belong to this affiliation. The head office is: Gîtes de France, 59 Rue Saint-Lazare, 75439 Paris-CEDEX 09, France, tel: 01.49.70.75.75, fax: 01.42.81.28.53, e-mail: info@gites-de-france.fr, website: www.gites-de-france.fr.

CREDIT CARDS

A few bed and breakfasts accept credit cards. When they do, we have indicated this in the description of the bed and breakfast using the following codes: AX–American Express, MC–MasterCard, VS–Visa, or simply, all major.

CURRENCY

Starting January 1999, 11 European countries (Austria, Belgium, Finland, France, Germany, Ireland, Italy, Luxembourg, Netherlands, Portugal, and Spain) had their currencies fixed to the new unit of European Monetary Union (EMU) currency, the euro. For the first three years the euro will be the internationally traded currency, though local currencies will remain in circulation. Then, during a six-month period beginning January 1, 2002, the euro will be phased in and local currencies will be phased out. Both types of currency will be valid during this six-month period. Finally, on July 1, 2002, local currencies will be removed from circulation.

DRIVING & DIRECTIONS

It is important to understand some basic directions in French when locating bed and breakfasts. Signs directing you to chambres d'hôtes are often accompanied by either *1ère à droite* (first road on the right) or *1ère à gauche* (first road on the left). Chambres d'Hôtes signs can vary from region to region, but most have adopted the national green-and-yellow sign of the Gîtes de France as shown on page 4.

Maps label the roads with their proper numbers, but you will find when driving that signs usually indicate a city direction instead of a road number. For example, instead of finding a sign for N909 north, you will see a sign for Lyon, so you must figure out by referring to your map whether Lyon is north of where you are and if N909 leads there. The city that is signposted is often a major city quite a distance away. This may seem awkward at first, but is actually an easy system once you adjust.

Most bed and breakfast homes and farmhouses are located outside the town or village under which they are listed. To make finding your destination easier, specific driving instructions are given in each bed and breakfast description. However, if you become lost while looking for your lodging, find the nearest post office or public phone box (usually in the central town square or in front of the post office) and call your hosts for directions. It is a good idea to keep a French telephone credit card handy for phone calls. In a pinch, bars and petrol stations will usually allow you to use their phones (they will charge you after the call). An added suggestion: Always plan to arrive at your destination before nightfall—road signs are difficult to see after dark.

ELECTRICAL CURRENT

If you are taking any electrical appliances made for use in the United States, you will need a transformer plus a two-pin adapter. A voltage of 220 AC current at 50 cycles per second is almost countrywide, though in remote areas you may encounter 120V. The voltage is often displayed on the socket. Even though we recommend that you purchase appliances with dual-voltage options whenever possible, it will still be necessary to have the appropriate socket adapter. Also, be especially careful with expensive equipment such as computers—verify with the manufacturer the adapter/converter capabilities and requirements.

LANGUAGE—LEVEL OF ENGLISH SPOKEN

Possessing even the most rudimentary knowledge and exposure to French will make your trip a thousand times more rewarding and enjoyable. Buy a French phrase book and a French/English dictionary before you leave home and do a little practicing. You can always get by: usually there is someone around who speaks at least a little English, and the French are accustomed to dealing with non-French-speaking travelers. It is helpful to carry paper and pencil to write down numbers for ease of comprehension, as well as a French phrase book and a French/English dictionary. If pronunciation seems to be a problem, you can then indicate the word or phrase in writing.

The level of English spoken in the bed and breakfasts in this guide runs the gamut from excellent to none at all. Because some of you will have fun practicing your high-school French while others will feel more comfortable communicating freely in English, we have indicated under each bed and breakfast description what you can expect. Levels of the hosts' English are indicated according to the following guidelines:

NO ENGLISH SPOKEN—a few words at best.

VERY LITTLE ENGLISH SPOKEN—a little more than the most rudimentary, or perhaps their children speak schoolroom English. More is understood than spoken.

SOME or GOOD ENGLISH SPOKEN—basic communication is possible, but longer, involved conversations are not. Speak slowly and clearly. Remember, they may understand more than they can articulate.

VERY GOOD ENGLISH SPOKEN—easy conversational English. More understood than able to express verbally.

FLUENT ENGLISH SPOKEN—can understand and communicate with ease—frequently the person has lived in Britain or the United States.

MAPS

Each itinerary is preceded by a map showing the route and each hotel listing is referenced on its top line to a map at the back of the book. In this guide there are 11 maps pinpointing the location of each bed and breakfast. To make it easier for you, hotel location maps are divided into a grid of four parts, a, b, c, and d, as indicated on each map's key. All maps are an artist's renderings and are not intended to replace detailed commercial maps. Places in the countryside are very tricky to find so it is vital that you supplement our maps with more detailed ones. Some of the best are those made by Michelin who publishes two sets of regional maps—we recommend and cross-reference the series numbered from 230 to 246. So that you will know what to purchase, we have put the corresponding Michelin map number at the bottom of each lodging description. Every bed and breakfast featured in this guide can be found on these maps. (Another bonus with the Michelin maps is that historical monuments are indicated and scenic routes are highlighted in green.) France B&B maps in this book can be cross-referenced with those in our companion guide, *France: Charming Inns & Itineraries*. We sell Michelin country maps, city maps, and regional green guides in our website store at *www.karenbrown.com*.

MEALS

BREAKFAST in a bed and breakfast is usually the Continental type, including a choice of coffee (black or with hot milk), tea, or hot chocolate, bread (sometimes a croissant or wheat bread for variety), butter, and jam. The evening before, hosts will customarily ask when you want breakfast and what beverage you prefer. Sometimes they will offer a choice of location such as outside in the garden or indoors in the dining area or kitchen.

TABLE D'HÔTE means that the host serves an evening meal. Of all the special features of a bed and breakfast experience, this is one of the most outstanding—if you see "Table d'hôte" offered under the bed and breakfast description, be sure to request it! You will not have a choice of menu, but you will have a delicious, home-cooked dinner (usually the ingredients are fresh from the garden) and be able to meet fellow guests. Most frequently meals are served at one large table with the hosts joining you and the other guests, but sometimes they are served at individual or shared tables. Expect at least three courses (an appetizer, a main course, and dessert), often four or five courses (with salad and cheese being served between the entree and dessert).

Prices quoted are **always** per person and sometimes include a table wine. The price depends upon how elaborate the meal is, the sophistication of the service, the number of courses, and what beverages are included. However, whether the meal is simple or gourmet, whenever you take advantage of the table d'hôte option, you will discover a real bargain and have a truly memorable experience. *Note:* The price for the meal might have increased before you arrive, so be sure to check.

When wine is included in the price of the meal, this is noted under the description. In a simple bed and breakfast, this is usually a house wine of the region—not fancy, but usually very good. Some of the deluxe places to stay often offer an aperitif before dinner, a selection of wines with the meal, and a nightcap afterwards.

There are a few places we recommend that, in addition to offering bed and breakfast accommodations, also have a restaurant. If so, this is noted in the description.

VERY IMPORTANT: When we indicate in the bed and breakfast description that table d'hôte is available, it is **always only available by prior arrangement**—and how often varies tremendously. Some bed and breakfasts offer table d'hôte every day; others serve dinner only when a minimum number of guests want to dine or on certain nights of the week. A few hosts seem to cook only when the whim strikes them. So, in other words—always take advantage of table d'hôte when it is offered, but be sure to check with your hosts to see if the option is available then make a dinner reservation when you book your room. Also inquire what time the meal will be served. Be sure to call your host from along the way if you are running late. The French do not have large freezers stocked with frozen supplies nor microwaves to defrost a quick meal. Food is usually fresh and purchased with care the day it is prepared, making it difficult to produce an impromptu meal. If you are a late arrival and have not eaten, sometimes your host will offer a plate of cold cuts, salad, and bread, but do not expect this, as it is not standard procedure. A few French terms to describe food services are listed below:

DEMI-PENSION includes breakfast and dinner with prices quoted per person. This usually saves you money.

PENSION COMPLÈTE includes breakfast, lunch, and dinner with prices quoted per person. This formula is rarely an option since most travelers prefer to be on their own for lunch.

FERME AUBERGE is a family-style restaurant, open to the public, on a working farm. These inns are actually controlled by the French government in so far as the products served must come mainly from the farm itself. The fare is usually simple and hearty, utilizing fresh meats and vegetables. The hosts do not generally sit down and share meals with their guests because they are often too busy serving.

PETS

If you miss your pet when on the road, bed and breakfast travel might be just your cup of tea. Even if not specifically mentioned in the write-up, chances are you will be greeted by a tail-wagging dog and often find a cat happily napping on the sofa. If you are traveling with your own pet, check to see if pets are accepted and what the charge will be when you make your reservation. The French love animals and some do allow you to bring your canine traveling companion.

RATES

In each bed and breakfast listing, 2000 summer rates are given for two persons in a double room, including tax, service, and Continental breakfast. Often rooms can accommodate up to four persons at additional charge and cribs and extra beds are usually available for children. Prices frequently go down if a stay is longer than three to five nights. Many places also offer small apartments or separate houses with cooking facilities that are ideal for families. Apartment rates do not include breakfast and are based on a week's stay (reservations are rarely accepted for periods of less than a week). Beautifully furnished country homes and castles can be real bargains although they will cost more if located in one of the prime tourist centers. Rates quoted were given to us at the time of publication and are subject to change. Be sure to verify the current price when making a reservation.

RESERVATIONS—GENERAL INFORMATION

A few bed and breakfasts in this guide offer a degree of sophistication that approaches that of a deluxe hotel. But remember the very essence of bed and breakfast accommodation is what makes it so special—these are private homes. It is not appropriate to just knock on the door and expect accommodation: prior reservations are essential. This also works to your advantage because most bed and breakfasts are tucked away in remote areas and it is frustrating to drive far out of your way, only to find everything is sold out. If you want to be footloose and not confined to a rigid schedule, phone from along the way to see if a room is available.

When making your reservations be sure to identify yourself as a *"Karen Brown Traveler."* We hear over and over again that the people who use our guides are such wonderful guests. The hotels appreciate your visit, value their inclusion in our guide, and frequently tell us they will take special care of our readers.

RESERVATIONS—DEPOSITS: Deposits are preferred if you are reserving several months ahead of your arrival date. Deposits are usually requested in French francs: this is for your own protection against fluctuating exchange rates. Drafts in French francs can be purchased at the main branch of many large banks. Credit cards are rarely accepted at bed and breakfasts, although they are sometimes accepted as a guarantee of arrival. Be aware that once you have paid your deposit, it is usually non-refundable.

RESERVATIONS BY E-MAIL: Gradually more and more bed and breakfasts are coming into the computer age and are adding an e-mail address. For those of you who know how to use the Internet, this is an inexpensive and convenient way to contact a hotel for a reservation. (See the reservation letter on page 14 for help.) *Note:* In any written correspondence be sure to spell out the month since Europeans reverse the American system for dates. As an example, in France 4/9/98 means September 4, not April 9.

RESERVATIONS BY FAX: The majority of bed and breakfasts have installed fax machines. If so, this is a very efficient way to request a reservation. (You can use our reservation letter). Be sure to spell out the month—see note in previous paragraph. For dialing instructions see "Reservations by Telephone."

RESERVATIONS BY MAIL: Writing a letter is the most popular method for booking accommodations, but allow plenty of time. It is advisable to write well in advance so that you will have time to write to your second choice if your first is unavailable. Allow at least a week each way for airmail to and from France. If you do not speak French, you can make a copy and use the reservation letter supplied on page 14. Be sure to spell out the month—see note in paragraph on e-mail.

RESERVATIONS BY TELEPHONE: If you speak French (or if we have indicated under the bed and breakfast description that fluent English is spoken by the owner), we recommend you call for a reservation. With a telephone call you can discuss what is available and most suited to your needs. It is best to always follow up with a letter and a deposit in French francs if requested. Telephone reservations are accepted by most bed and breakfast homes, but if there is a language barrier, it will be frustrating and difficult to communicate your wants. (Remember the time difference when calling: Paris is six hours ahead of New York.) To place a call, dial the international code (011 from the United States), then the country code for France (33) followed by the telephone number (dropping the initial 0). If dialing within France, dial the initial 0.

RESERVATIONS & CHECK-IN: Bed and breakfasts are not hotels—they are private homes. There is not always someone "at the front desk" to check you in, so it is courteous to call the day you are expected to reconfirm your reservation, and to advise what time you anticipate arriving. If you have made arrangements to dine, ask what hour dinner will be served and be sure to be on time.

RESERVATIONS & CANCELLATIONS: If it is necessary for you to cancel your reservation for any reason, please phone (or write far in advance) to alert the proprietor. Bed and breakfasts often have only a few rooms to rent and are thus severely impacted financially if they hold a room for a "no-show."

TELEPHONES

TELEPHONES—HOW TO CALL WITHIN FRANCE: It is very important to know how to make telephone calls within France. There are no longer any coin phones in France. The public telephones accept only special credit cards and although at first this seems complicated, it is actually easy. Stop by a post office (*bureau de poste*), a newsstand (*bureau de tabac*), or a highway gas station and buy a credit card for a specified amount of credit. You place this card into a slot in the telephone; then, when you complete your call, the cost is automatically subtracted from the total available credit.

TELEPHONES—HOW TO CALL THE USA: Unlike hotels, most bed and breakfasts rarely have direct-dial telephones in the guestrooms. If your hosts do not have a telephone you can use, public telephones are readily available. The best bet is to use an international telephone card from your long-distance company—with one of these you can make a local call within France and be connected with your USA operator (ask your long-distance carrier what access number to use).

TOURIST INFORMATION

Syndicat d'Initiative is the name for the tourist offices found in all towns and resorts in France. When you are on the road, it is very helpful to pop into one of these offices signposted with a large "I". The agents gladly give advice on local events, timetables for local trains, buses and boats, and often have maps and brochures on the region's points of interest. They can also help with locating bed and breakfast accommodations. Before you depart for France, call their general information number in the USA at (410) 286-8310 or visit their website: www.fgtousa.org. Additional information can be obtained by writing or faxing one of the tourist offices listed below:

French Government Tourist Offices:

444 Madison Ave., 16th Floor, New York, NY 10022-6903, USA, fax: (212) 838-7855

9454 Wilshire Blvd., Suite 715, Beverly Hills, CA 90212-2967, USA, fax: (310) 276-2835

676 N. Michigan Ave., Suite 3360, Chicago, IL 60611-2819, USA, fax: (312) 337-6339

178 Piccadilly, London W1V OAL, England, fax: (020) 7493-6594

1981 Avenue McGill College, Suite 490, Montreal, PQ H3A 2W9, Canada, fax: (514) 845-4868

WEBSITE

We are constantly changing and updating the Karen Brown website with the aim of providing an enhanced extension of our guides and supplying you with even more information on the properties and destinations that we recommend. Many hotels that we work very closely with are featured on our website—their web addresses are detailed on the description pages. In 2000 we will continue to add photos for as many properties as possible and you will be able to link directly to the hotels' individual websites, if available, for their personal photos and more information. On our site we share comments, feedback, and discoveries from you, our readers, and keep you informed of our latest finds, current updates, and special offers. We want our website to serve as a valuable and added dimension to our guides. Be sure to visit us at www.karenbrown.com.

Reservation Letter

To: Bed and Breakfast, name and address

Monsieur/Madame:

Nous serons _____ personnes.
We have (number) of persons in our party

Nous voudrions réserver pour _____ nuit(s)
We would like to reserve for (number of nights)

    du _____
    from (date of arrival)

    au _____
    to (date of departure),

    une chambre à deux lits _____
    a room(s) with twin beds

    une chambre au grand lit _____
    a room(s) with double bed(s)

    une chambre avec un lit supplémentaire _____
    room(s) with an extra bed

    avec toilette et baignoire ou douche privée _____
    with private toilet and bathtub or shower

Veuilliez confirmer la réservation en nous communicant le prix de la chambre et la somme d'arrhes que vous souhaitez. Dans l'attente de votre réponse, nous vous prions d'agréer, Messieurs, Mesdames, l'expression de nos sentiments distingués.

Please advise availability, rate of room and deposit needed. We will be waiting for your confirmation and send our kindest regards.

Your name and address and fax number (if applicable)

Bed & Breakfast Descriptions

Harry Lammot Belin (who is from the United States) owns the Château Andelot, but do not worry—this is not a castle bought on a whim by a wealthy American wanting to pretend to be Lord of the Manor—the property is his family home. It was Harry's grandfather who returned to the beautiful Jura region in *La France Profonde* many years ago with his cousin Pierre du Pont looking for their roots and purchased one of their 12th-century ancestral castles, Château Andelot, as a holiday abode. When Harry came into the picture, the castle's interior was deteriorating. His solution was to bring the château back to its former glory and recover some of the staggering costs of renovation by opening it as a bed and breakfast. Today the guest enjoys an intimate, picture-perfect, stone fort, approached through an original 12th century gate, fortified by a pair of turreted towers. From the courtyard (and also from within the château) there are sweeping vistas of rolling forested hills and valleys. The interior is as stunning as it is comfortable: elegant antique furnishings (mostly purchased by Harry's grandfather) are enhanced by sumptuous fabrics in rich colors, all put together by his wife Susan. *Directions:* The château is about midway between Bourg en Bresse and Lons le Saunier. Leave the A39 at the Beaupont exit, 8 km west of St. Amour, or the N83 at St. Amour and take the D3 east towards St. Julien via Nanc and Thoissia. After 12 km, just before village of Andelot, the château is signposted on your left.

CHÂTEAU ANDELOT (Gîtes de France)
Hosts: Susan & Harry Lammot Belin
Rue de l'Eglise
39320 Andelot-les St. Amour, France
Tel: 03.84.85.41.49, Fax: 03.84.85.46.74
E-mail: chateau-andelot@wanadoo.fr
6 rooms, Double: 950F, Suite: 1,295F
Table d'hôte: 220F per person (beverages not included)
Open all year, Credit cards: all major, Fluent English spoken
Region: Jura, Michelin Map 243
www.karenbrown.com/france/chateauandelot.html

Although Les Hêtres Rouges is located in Burgundy, it was never associated with wine growing. Its ancestry was that of a hunting lodge—many forests still abound where wild boar roam. Wrought-iron gates lead into a large park and the pretty peach-colored 18th-century manor house with gray-blue shutters. An old wooden staircase twists up to the bedrooms which are romantically tucked up under the eaves. Each bedroom is lovingly decorated by your charming hostess, Christiane Bugnet, with antique furniture and pretty Laura Ashley fabrics. Christiane is an artist who paints in the vibrant colors of the countryside, which she also used throughout in her decor. My favorite bedroom overlooks the back garden and is painted yellow with a pretty floral print on the bedspreads and curtains. If you are planning to use Les Hêtres Rouges as a hub to explore this glorious region of France, splurge and request the suite. Here you have your own romantic, two-story, ivy-covered cottage, adorable with pink shutters (adorned with heart-shaped cutouts), its own kitchen, and a private little garden terrace where breakfast is served. *Directions:* Located between Beaune and Dijon. From the autoroute A31, take the Nuit-Saint-Georges exit. Almost as soon as you exit the highway, follow the signs that lead back over the expressway towards Seurre. After 3 km, turn right towards Quincey. Go through Quincey and continue on for 4 km to Artilly. As you arrive in Artilly, watch for the Chambres d'Hôtes sign on the right, marking the entrance to Les Hêtres Rouges.

LES HÊTRES ROUGES (Gîtes de France)
Hostess: Christiane Bugnet
Antilly, 21700 Argilly, France
Tel: 03.80.62.53.98, Fax:03.80.62.54.85
4 rooms, Double: 450F–600F
No table d'hôte
Open Mar to Nov, Some English spoken
Region: Burgundy, Michelin Map 243
www.karenbrown.com/france/leshetresrouges.html

A country lane delivers you to the doorstep of Les Aubépines, a true working farm nestled on lush acreage. This cozy and intimate timbered brick farmhouse has a fairytale appearance—windows are shuttered, dormers pop through the angles and pitches of the second-story roof, and the front façade is stacked high with firewood. When we arrived, Yves was mowing his vast acreage of lawn but was not too busy to give us a warm welcome and an offer of refreshing cider. We found Françoise inside and settled with her in front of the open fire in the main salon, a very inviting room with windows opening on to the surrounding greenery and heavy old beams hung with a melange of pottery, copper pots, and fresh flowers. The Closson-Mazes offer table d'hôte to guests on a pre-arranged basis, using regional as well as many homegrown products. An open stairwell climbs from the main room to a comfy loft sitting area (with television) and two guestrooms. Both are attractive: the pink room has a shower and the yellow room enjoys the privacy of its own back stair and has a private bath. At the other end of the hallway is a suite of rooms, which affords a family private, comfortable living space. *Directions:* 13 km southeast of Pont Audemer. Coming from Paris, take the A13 to exit 26 towards Pont Audemer. After 2 km at the Medine roundabout, take D89 towards Evreux. Turn left immediately after the Les Marettes sign towards Rondemare, then continue straight, following signs to Les Chauffourniers and Chambres d'Hôtes.

"LES AUBÉPINES" AUX CHAUFFOURNIERS   **New**
Hosts: Françoise & Yves Closson-Maze
27290 Appeville dit Annebault, France
Tel & fax: 02.32.56.14.25
3 rooms, Double: 270F–470F
Table d'hôte: 110F per person, wine not included
Open Apr. to Sep. and off season by reservation
Fluent English spoken
Region: Normandy, Michelin Map: 231

Le Petit Romieu is situated in an intriguing part of France, a wild, open, unpopulated region of flatlands and marshes that stretch from Arles to the sea. You see some brilliant green rice fields, but this is also a region of vast estates where champion bulls are bred for the bullring and wild horses roam free. We love this open country and were happy to discover here a bed and breakfast, Le Petit Romieu. The home is very appealing—a two-story, creamy-toned stone building with tall French doors on the ground level and tall windows above, all attractively framed with light-blue shutters. A terrace dotted with white chairs and tables plus a green lawn bordered by rose bushes complete the attractive scene. There are a dining room and a couple of guest lounges on the first floor and then a staircase winds up to the bedrooms, each of which is individually decorated using pretty fabrics. The table d'hôte is a wonderful meal served family-style around one large table. *Directions*: From A54, take the Arles exit 4 marked to Les Saintes Maries de la Mer on the D570. After about 3 km, turn left on D36 marked to Salin de Giraud. After about 3 km more, turn right on D36B marked to Gageron and continue until you come to the hamlet of Villeneuve. At the intersection follow the road marked to Fielouse. Turn left on a lane signposted Le Petit Romieu. Do not turn in at the large manor on the left (this is the owner's home). Instead, continue on following the small Le Petit Romieu signs to the bed and breakfast.

LE PETIT ROMIEU   **New**
Host: M. Blanchet
Villeneuve
13200 Arles, France
Tel: 04.90.97.00.27, Fax: 04.90.97.00.52
5 rooms, Double: 450F
Table d'hôte: 100F per person, includes wine
Open Mar to Sep, 2-night minimum
No English spoken
Region: Camargue, Michelin Maps 245, 246

A breathtakingly lovely Renaissance castle, the Château de la Verrerie offers the comfort and refinement of an English country home coupled with incomparable French flair for artful decoration and fine cuisine. Each guest bedroom is spacious and unique, with its own color scheme and special charm. For example, one room is done in shades of rose, complemented by a gray marble fireplace and fine antique furnishings. A writing desk placed near the window overlooks the well-manicured lawns and gardens which extend to nearby woods. The adjoining spacious bathroom comes complete with claw-footed tub. An inviting guest sitting room combines warmth and elegance to a perfect degree, offering plenty of comfortable seating, good lighting, and reading materials in several languages. In addition to relaxing in this esthetically beautiful setting, you can also tour the historic chapel and Renaissance gallery and enjoy gourmet lunches and dinners served in the nearby Auberge d'Helène. This restaurant, found in a cozy and atmospheric 18th-century cottage, features regional dishes and fine wines. *Directions:* Located 76 km southeast of Orléans and 44 km northeast of Bourges. From Bourges travel north on the D940 for 34 km. At La Chapelle d'Angillon travel northeast on D926 for 6 km to Le Grand Rond. La Verrerie, 4 km north, is reached by following D39 and D89.

CHÂTEAU DE LA VERRERIE
Hosts: Comte & Comtesse Béraud de Vogüé
Oizon, 18700 Aubigny-sur-Nère, France
Tel: 02.48.81.51.60, Fax: 02.48.58.21.25
E-mail: laverrerie@wanadoo.fr
12 rooms, Double: 900–1,300F, breakfast not included
Table d'hôte: 390F per person
Closed Christmas, Credit cards: all major
Fluent English spoken
Region: Centre, Michelin Map 238
www.karenbrown.com/france/chateaudelaverrerie.html

La Bihourderie was once home to the "Bohor," who trained the knights at jousting tournaments during the Middle Ages. La Bihourderie is a long, low farmhouse draped in ivy and full of character. White shuttered windows peek out from this picturesque one-story home, further enhanced by a very steep roof which is prettily accented by gabled windows. This is a family home and Mignès Bouin and her family are gracious hosts. La Bihourderie is extremely appealing, and makes a well-priced base for visiting the fabulous châteaux of the Loire Valley. The tidy front courtyard of this working farm abounds with beautifully tended, colorful flower gardens. There is a separate section of the house with a private parlor just for the guests, off which you find the four bedrooms, named after works of art by Van Gogh. Les Iris is attractively decorated with fabrics blending with the framed copy of Van Gogh's painting of the iris and Les Blés Jaunes has clever touches of tied wheat bunches and a painted frieze. Everything is exceptionally well kept and immaculately clean. When the days are warm, both breakfast and dinner are served at tables set outside on the lawn behind the house, so wonderfully close to the fields. Crops alternate with each year from wheat to sunflowers. I hope you're there when the sunflowers are in full bloom coloring the miles of acreage yellow. *Directions:* From Tours, take the N143 towards Loches. Go through Cormery, then turn left 10 km after Cormery in the direction of Azay-sur-Indre. The Chambres d'Hôtes sign is on your left.

LA BIHOURDERIE (*Gîtes de France*)
Hosts: Mignès & Christophe Bouin
37310 Azay-sur-Indre, France
Tel: 02.47.92.58.58, Fax: 02.47.92.22.19
4 rooms, Double: 240F–260F
Table d'hôte: 85F per person, includes wine
Open all year, Good English spoken
Region: Loire Valley, Michelin Map 238
www.karenbrown.com/france/labihourderie.html

Arlette Vachet's English-style country cottage is at the top of our list for romantic and atmospheric bed and breakfast accommodation. Arlette is a painter and former antique dealer who has filled her cozy, ivy-covered house with a potpourri of country antiques and used her artistic talents to decorate the interior to charming perfection. Her salon is a virtual treasure trove of paintings, old furniture and objets d'art, set off by low, beamed ceilings and an old stone hearth. A comfortable couch and a crackling fire are the perfect accompaniments to an evening's aperitif before sampling one of the region's many restaurants, renowned for their fine wines and gourmet cuisine. French doors open from the garden to the ground-floor bedroom, prettily decorated in a butterfly motif in tones of forest green and pink. In addition to the first-floor room, there are two bedrooms upstairs—one small and intimate with a low, sloping ceiling covered by beautiful flowered wallpaper, the other a small suite. In addition, across the garden is a most engaging cottage for guests who want to stay a week. *Directions:* Baudrières is located 19 km southeast of Châlon-sur-Saône. From the A6 (Paris to Lyon) take the Châlon South exit. Follow the green signs saying "Lyon bis." Go through Epervans and Ouroux-sur-Saône on D 978, then turn right on D 933 towards Simandre. After 2 km turn left at Nassey to Baudrières. La Chaumière is located across from the church.

LA CHAUMIÈRE (Gîtes de France)
Hostess: Arlette Vachet
Baudrières
71370 Saint Germain du Plain, France
Tel: 03.85.47.32.18, Fax: 03.85.47.41.42
Cellphone: 06.07.43.53.46
2 rooms, 1 suite, Double: 350F, Suite: 450F
No table d'hôte
Open all year, Good English spoken
Region: Burgundy, Michelin Map 243
www.karenbrown.com/france/lachaumiere.html

Ludovic and Eliane Cornillon have struck the perfect balance between rustic ambiance and luxurious comfort in their charming farmhouse found in the countryside of northern Provence. The entire farm complex dates from 1769 and is rectangular in shape, forming a tranquil central garden sheltered by weathered stone walls. A low doorway leads into the historic entry salon which has a large old hearth decorated with dried flower bouquets and interesting antique furniture including a *pétrai*, a piece somewhat like a large chest used for both storing flour and kneading bread dough. The adjoining dining room, formerly the stables, still displays a stone feeding trough and a little stairway leading to the attic where the hay was stored. Eliane's fresh style of cuisine features regional herbs and is complemented well by Domaine de Saint Luc wines, as Ludovic is a talented wine maker. After dinner, a good night's rest is assured in charming bedrooms, all with spotless private baths. There is also a swimming pool near the house for guests' use. *Directions:* La Baume de Transit is located about 24 km north of Orange. Take autoroute A7 and exit at Bollène, following directions for Suze La Rousse on D94. Leave Suze La Rousse on D59 towards Saint Paul Trois Châteaux, but turn off almost immediately onto the small country road CD117 towards La Baume de Transit. Look for signs for Domaine de Saint Luc.

DOMAINE DE SAINT LUC (Gîtes de France)
Hosts: Eliane & Ludovic Cornillon
Le Gas du Rossignol, La Baume de Transit
26130 Saint Paul-Trois Châteaux, France
Tel: 04.75.98.11.51, Fax: 04.75.98.19.22
6 rooms, Double: 390F
Table d'hôte: 145F per person
Closed Dec, Good English spoken by Eliane
Region: Provence, Michelin Map 245

In the hills near Toulon, the Zerbibs opened their lovely home as a bed and breakfast. Marceau Zerbib, a talented architect, completely renovated the house so that there are now four attractive guest bedrooms, tastefully appointed in a quiet, elegant manner with country antiques enhanced by lovely fabrics. The home (a traditional Provençal-style structure with a heavy tiled roof and green shutters) has a parklike setting that is captivating. The gardens are spectacular, with a lush lawn sweeping away behind the house to steps leading down to a lower terrace with a large pool surrounded by comfortable lounge chairs. Overlooking the pool is a protected terrace and a cheerful blue-and-white tiled outdoor kitchen where guests may prepare a light meal. Well-tended gardens abound—the display of flowers everywhere is magnificent. In the background the property extends to a backdrop of pine and olive trees. Neither Charlotte nor Marceau speaks English, but their hospitality is so genuine that language barriers are quickly overcome. *Directions:* From the A50 (about 11 km west of Toulon), take the Bandol exit and follow signs to Le Beausset on the D559. Go through the village and take the second right at the roundabout. In about a block you see a Casino supermarket on your left and on your right a *boulangerie*. Take the tiny road beside the bakery (Chemin de Cinq-Sous) for 1.1 km. Turn left at a small lane signposted Zerbib, Marceau-Architect and continue a short distance to Les Cancades.

LES CANCADES (Gîtes de France)
Hosts: Charlotte & Marceau Zerbib
83330 Le Beausset, France
Tel: 04.94.98.76.93, Fax: 04.94.90.24.63
E-mail: charlotte.zerbib@wanadoo.fr
4 rooms, Double: 350F–400F
No table d'hôte
Open all year, No English spoken
Region: Côte d'Azur, Michelin Map 245
www.karenbrown.com/france/lescancades.html

Les Tournillayres is an especially delightful bed and breakfast. Every detail—from the beautifully tended gardens to the impeccably maintained guestrooms—displays the hand of a meticulous, caring owner. There is a refreshing mood of naturalness about the property which is dotted with olive trees and green oaks, and bounded by vineyards—nothing seems stiff or formal. Your lovely hostess, Marie Claire, lives with her family on the grounds in a picture-perfect farmhouse with pink stucco exterior, pretty blue shutters, and rustic red-tiled roof. Tucked in the gardens and scented by lavender are four sweet individual cottages which, like the main house, are a pretty, soft pink accented by blue shutters and doors. Each spacious cottage has been charmingly decorated in a cozy French-country style. The furnishings are similar throughout—only the fabrics and color schemes vary. All the rooms have twin beds, beamed ceiling, hand-crafted fireplace, antique tiles, a small kitchen, and a private terrace where guests enjoy the breakfast Marie Claire delivers each morning, packaged in a pretty picnic basket. *Directions:* From Carpentras take D974 northeast for 15 km to Bédoin. Go through town and continue on D974 marked to Mont Ventoux. Just as the road leaves Bédoin, watch for a tiny Les Tournillayres sign on your right and a service garage on your left. Turn left and continue to follow signs for Les Tournillayres—about 2 km from Bédoin.

LES TOURNILLAYRES (*Gîtes de France*)
Hostess: Marie Claire Renaudon
84410 Bédoin, France
Tel & fax: 04.90.12.80.94
4 cottages, Double: from 450F, Suite: 600F (4 persons)
No table d'hôte
Open Mar to mid-Nov, Very little English spoken
Children up to 4 accepted
Region: Provence, Michelin Map 245
www.karenbrown.com/france/lestournillayres.html

Betschdorf is a picturesque, half-timbered town that has always been known for its distinctive blue-toned stoneware. Traditional pottery methods are handed down from generation to generation, and host Christian Krumeich represents the ninth generation of potters in his family. He and his artistic wife, Joelle, have installed charming guest quarters above their large pottery workshop, offering the traveler independent, stylish accommodations. Rooms are small yet very attractive, furnished in highly tasteful combinations of contemporary and antique furniture. Artful decor includes pastel upholstery, Monet prints, dried-flower arrangements, and colorful durrie rugs. The guest salon, decorated with Oriental rugs, antique furniture, well-chosen objets d'art, and bookshelves stocked with interesting reading, offers a refined, comfortable ambiance for relaxation and meals. *Directions:* Betschdorf is located approximately 44 km northeast of Strasbourg. Take N63 past Hagenau, continuing on D263 towards Hunspach and Wissembourg. After about 10 km, turn right onto D243 to Betschdorf. Soon after entering town, on the main street, look for the Krumeichs' driveway on the right, marked by a sign for Poterie and Chambres d'Hôtes.

CHEZ KRUMEICH (Gîtes de France)
Hosts: Joelle & Christian Krumeich
23, Rue des Potiers
67660 Betschdorf, France
Tel: 03.88.54.40.56, Fax: 03.88.54.47.67
3 rooms, Double: 290F–320F
No table d'hôte
Open all year, Credit cards: MC, VS
Some English spoken by Joelle
Region: Alsace, Michelin Map 242
www.karenbrown.com/france/chezkrumeich.html

La Grande Métairie, a characterful 16th-century stone farmhouse, belonged to Christine Moy's grandfather. Happily, very little has been altered over the years except for the necessary modernization of plumbing and electricity. The beamed-ceilinged dining room is a gem. Its enormous fireplace, copper pots, fresh flowers, antique fruitwood sideboard, and stone floors gleaming with the patina of age are enhanced by meter-thick walls. Here Christine sets the table with a checkered cloth and serves on beautiful Limoges china. Breakfast consists of homemade breads, yogurt, cheeses and jams. There are two tastefully decorated bedrooms plus a two-bedroom apartment. La Grande Métairie is a simple working farm. The accommodations, ambiance, and genuine warmth of welcome far outshine the modest price (there is even a swimming pool on a back terrace). *Directions:* Ruffec is located 147 km northeast of Bordeaux via the N10. Go to Ruffec and take D740 east towards Confolens. After the road crosses the river, take D197 towards Bioussac, then in 1.3 km turn left towards Oyer. Soon you will see La Grande Métairie on your left. *Note:* Trains run from Paris to Ruffec each day (6 km from the farm).

LA GRANDE MÉTAIRIE (Gîtes de France)
Hosts: Christine & Jean Louis Moy
Oyer, 16700 Bioussac, France
Tel: 05.45.31.15.67, Fax: 05.45.29.07.28
2 rooms, Double: 230F, 1 apt: 2,250F per week (4 pers)
No table d'hôte
Open Apr to Nov, Very good English spoken
Region: Limousin, Michelin Map 233
www.karenbrown.com/france/lagrandemetairie.html

If you want to experience genuine French hospitality in a storybook château, the Château de Brie is perfection. Hosts Comte and Comtesse du Manoir de Juaye's welcome is so warm, so genuine, that you quickly feel right at home. The castle was used for many years only for holidays, but now it is the family's permanent home and although the four daughters live away, they too love the château and come home as often as possible. The rooms of the castle are elegant yet comfortable. The furnishings are gorgeous—all family antiques that have been in the castle forever. One of the most endearing qualities of this castle is that although the walls are 2 meters thick, light streams through the many windows, giving the rooms a light and cheerful ambiance. The Château de Brie is surrounded by pretty gardens and grassy lawns that stretch out behind the castle—in every direction there are tranquil views of trees and farmland. Beyond the manicured park (dominated by the picture-perfect castle) the family owns 1,000 acres of forest, a haven for walking. Tennis courts, a swimming pool, and bicycles are also available for guests' use. As an added bonus guests can enjoy a special mechanical puppet show in the barn. *Directions:* Brie is located 45 km southwest of Limoges. From Limoges go southwest on N21 for 35 km. Exit at Chalus and follow the D42 west towards Cussac. In about 8 km you see the Château de Brie well signposted on the right side of the road.

CHÂTEAU DE BRIE (Gîtes de France)
Hosts: Comte & Comtesse Pierre du Manoir de Juaye
Brie, 87150 Champagnac La Riviere, France
Tel: 05.55.78.17.52, Fax: 05.55.78.14.02
E-mail: chateaudebrie@wanadoo.fr
4 rooms, Double: 550F–650F
Table d'hôte: 250F per person, includes wine
Open Apr to Nov (by reservations rest of year)
Fluent English spoken
Region: Limousin, Michelin Map 233
www.karenbrown.com/france/chateaudebrie.html

The Château de la Bourgonie combines all the ingredients to make a stay in France unforgettable: a fabulous old stone château dating back to the 14th century, breathtaking antiques, stunning decor, and a marvelously interesting history. As if this wasn't enough, the owners, Christine and Hubert de Commarque, open their hearts as well as their home to their guests. The château is a quadrangle built around a large central courtyard. One wing can be used as a complete home with kitchen, dining room, living room, and four bedrooms (perfect for stays of a week or more) or the four bedrooms are available on a bed and breakfast basis. When I asked Christine how long the château had been in her family, the answer was very simple, "forever." Just a short drive away, perched on a hillside above the River Dordogne, the de Commarque family owns the Château de la Poujade, an equally gorgeous home available to rent by the week. Either of the châteaux you choose offers peace and utter tranquillity near the prehistoric caves of Lascaux and the medieval town of Sarlat. In fact, the family has its own caves on their family property in Les Eyzies, which is open to the public (free to guests). *Directions:* Le Buisson is located 128 km east of Bordeaux. From Le Buisson take D25 towards Siorac. As you leave Le Buisson, take the first road to the right. It goes over the railroad tracks and up the hill. The road splits twice—each time go left. The road dead-ends at Château de la Bourgonie.

CHÂTEAU DE LA BOURGONIE
Hosts: Christine & Hubert de Commarque
Paleyrac, 24480 Le Buisson, France
Tel: 05.53.22.01.78, Fax: 05.53.27.97.67
4 rooms, Double: 750F, 4-bedroom apt: 9,000F per week
No table d'hôte
Open Apr to Nov, Fluent English spoken
Region: Dordogne, Michelin Map 235
www.karenbrown.com/france/chateaudelabourgonie.html

The Manoir des Tourpes (a beautiful, pastel-ochre manor accented by gray slate roof) is only 15 kilometers from Caen, yet sets a mood of being deep in the countryside. The lush lawn with a lazy weeping willow tree is bounded on two sides by a stone fence banked by beautifully tended flowerbeds. The third side of the property is traced by the River Dives. Beyond the river, open marshlands (dotted with cows and sheep) sweep to distant rolling hills. A comfortable parlor is set aside exclusively for the use of guests. Steps lead to the attractively furnished bedrooms. My favorite is the red room: it isn't the largest, but it's terribly romantic. Tucked under the sloping roof, it has a beamed ceiling, pretty red carpet, double bed with patchwork quilt made by Michael's mother, and a charming antique writing desk set in front of casement windows overlooking the meandering river. The gracious owner, Michael Cassady, was born in the United States but has lived in France for many years. He and his lovely French-born wife, Marie-Catherine, lived in Paris before moving to Normandy. The charm, ambiance, and comfort of their delightful home far exceed what you would expect for such a modest room price. *Directions:* From Paris, take exit 29b (Dozulé) off the A13, and follow signs to Troarn on the N175. At Troarn, turn right on the D95. Go 2 km to Bures-sur-Dives and follow signs to the Manoir (near the church). From Caen, take exit 30.

MANOIR DES TOURPES (*Gîtes de France*)
Hosts: Michael Cassady & Marie-Catherine Landon
3 Rue de l'Église
14670 Bures-sur-Dives, France
Tel: 02.31.23.63.47, Fax: 02.31.23.86.10
E-mail: mcassady@mail.cpod.fr
3 rooms, Double: 300F–390F, No table d'hôte
Open mid-Mar to mid-Nov, Fluent English spoken
Region: Normandy, Michelin Map 231
www.karenbrown.com/france/manoirdestourpes.html

In 1975 Corinne and Régis Burckel de Tell bought a characterful 15th-century stone house facing directly onto the main street in the center of Calvisson, a very old village surrounded by vineyards just west of Nîmes. Corinne (an art historian) and Régis (an artist) were passionately committed to preserving the architecture and culture of the area and began the tremendous task of authentically restoring the mansion. Ceilings were stripped back to expose original beams, floors covered with stone slabs or terra-cotta tiles, and fireplaces brought back to working order. When finished with the construction, they furnished the house with a charming rustic simplicity. Nothing is cluttered or contrived—country antiques and natural fabrics prevail throughout. In the heart of the house is a romantic courtyard garden which is a true delight, with flowers and greenery setting off the stone walls. It is here under the stars that dinner is usually served. When the weather is chilly, guests eat family-style at one large table in a wonderful room with stone walls and arched ceiling. The bedrooms, reached by a stone-slab circular staircase, are individually furnished and display the same tasteful, understated beauty. Régis, whose paintings highlight the walls throughout the house, offers week-long art classes for small groups. *Directions:* From A9, take the Gallargues exit then the N113 towards Nîmes. Take the D1 to Calvisson just after the Bas Rhône Canal. Once in the village follow the signs to the house, which is two doors from the Town Hall going up the hill.

CHEZ BURCKEL DE TELL
Hosts: Corinne & Régis Burckel de Tell
Grand Rue 48, 30420 Calvisson, France
Tel: 04.66.01.23.91, Fax: 04.66.01.42.19
6 rooms, Double: 280F, Suite: 350F
Table d'hôte: 80F per person, includes wine
Open all year, Very good English spoken
Region: Midi, Michelin Map 240
www.karenbrown.com/france/chezburckeldetell.html

From the moment you enter Domaine de la Picquoterie it is apparent that this enchanting, 13th-century stone farmhouse is the home of an artist. Each view captures a well-thought-out scene, so perfect, yet so natural, it is like a painting. The charming owner, Jean-Gabriel Laloy, is an artist whose skills extend beyond his canvases. He rebuilt the long-neglected farmhouse, designed the incredibly beautiful gardens, upholstered the furniture, and sewed the drapes. As if these talents were not enough, a neighbor introduced him to needlepoint. As you enter, a massive stone fireplace sets the theme for the charming, intimate parlor with terra-cotta floors, massive beamed ceiling, stone walls, and a soft beige-and-white color scheme. Upstairs, two bedrooms display a timeless, restful decor of beiges, creams, and whites. All the materials are of natural fabrics with off-white homespun drapes and chairs, and soft-beige walls. The quiet tone-on-tone color scheme of the bedrooms is dramatically accented by the view out of the windows of colorful flowerbeds and an expanse of manicured green lawn. Jean-Gabriel's paintings are lovely, but his masterpiece is certainly the lovely home and award-winning garden he has created. For a romantic stay consider the delightful two-bedroom suite. *Directions:* Domaine de la Picquoterie is off the RN13 between Cherbourg and Bayeux. Exit the RN13 at Saint-Pierre du Mont, D204. Afterwards, follow signs for La Picquoterie.

DOMAINE DE LA PICQUOTERIE
Host: Jean-Gabriel Laloy
14230 La Cambe, France
Tel: 02.31.92.09.82, Fax: 02.31.51.90.91
Cellphone: 06.62.09.09.82
3 rooms, 1-bedroom cottage
Double: 650F, Suite: from 1,200F, Cottage (2-night min): 500F
No table d'hôte, No smoking, No pets, Credit cards: MC, VS
Open all year with reservations, Good English spoken
Region: Normandy, Michelin Map 231
www.karenbrown.com/france/domainedelapicquoterie.html

This handsome brick and timbered farm complex dates back to 1610 and its architecture is unusual, with interesting angles, peaks, and pitches to its steep slate roof. You enter into a grand tiled and paneled hall with a great wooden staircase that climbs to the second-floor guestrooms. Just beyond the entry is the magnificent dining room with an intricate mural encircling the room at the top of the wall and one large table set under high, wide beams beautifully painted 200 years ago and in front of a large open fireplace. Served in the dining room, breakfast is the traditional French repast of breads, jams, and beverages, adapted to suit different nationality and culinary requests. The three guestrooms are all quite spacious and are named for their color schemes. The Green Room is south facing and will have its own bathroom by the time this book goes to press (at the time of our visit it had a private bath downstairs). The Yellow Room, a corner room with windows facing both to the south and west, was especially pretty and spacious and enjoys a large private bathroom. The Rose Room is pretty in its rose-and-cream print and has a beautiful view across the acres of pasture. Handsome armoires, lovely antique beds, and comfortable chairs decorate each room and they all enjoy the quiet of the farm setting. *Directions:* From Caen: Take the N13 in the direction of Lisieux. At the crossroads of Carrefour St. Jean take the D50 for 5 km. The manor is on the right just past (east of) the intersection of the D85 to Cambremer.

MANOIR DE CANTEPIE   **New**
Hosts: Christine & Arnauld Gherrak
14340 Cambremer, France
Tel: 02.31.62.87.27, Fax: none
3 rooms, Double: 300F
No table d'hôte
Open all year
Very good English spoken
Region: Normandy, Michelin Map: 231

The Château du Foulon, built in 1840, is a beautiful small château, owned by Vicomte and Vicomtesse de Baritault du Carpia. The home is surrounded by a 100-acre park, complete with 25 handsome peacocks and one naughty swan. Inside, the rooms without exception are furnished with exquisite antiques, many dating back to the 17th century. The essence within is of a fine home, elegant, yet very comfortable, with an appealing, lived-in ambiance—photographs of beautiful children and grandchildren prove this is indeed a family dwelling, The guestrooms, each nicely decorated with pretty wallpapers and attractive fabrics, look out over the gardens from large casement windows. In addition to the five bedrooms, there are also two charming apartments, each with its own little kitchen, bedroom, and living room. These would make an excellent choice for accommodation if you plan to stay for an extended time. There are few homes in the Médoc that open their doors as a bed and breakfast, so it is a pleasure to recommend the Château du Foulon. If you want to explore the glorious Médoc (which produces some of the world's finest wines) or just enjoy an interlude in the French countryside, this lovely château makes an excellent choice. *Directions:* Take D1 north from Bordeaux for about 28 km. When you reach Castelnau de Médoc, at the first traffic light turn left and almost immediately you see the sign for Château du Foulon on your left.

CHÂTEAU DU FOULON
Hosts: Vicomte & Vicomtesse de Baritault du Carpia
33480 Castelnau de MédocFrance
Tel: 05.56.58.20.18, Fax: 05.56.58.23.43
5 rooms, 2 apts, Double: 450F–600F, Apt: 500F–600F
No table d'hôte
Open all year, Very little English spoken
Region: Médoc, Michelin Map 233
www.karenbrown.com/france/chateaudufoulon.html

When Lois and Terry Link decided to retire, France was a natural choice. Not only had their hearts been drawn to France for many years, but also their son had married a French woman. Lois (a gourmet chef who owned a cheese shop in San Francisco) and Terry (a journalist for 20 years at the *Oakland Tribune*) bought a wonderful old *boulangerie* (bakery) in a picturesque village near Carcassonne. The bread-selling area is now a little cozy sitting room, very comfortable and inviting with Provençal print fabrics combined with cheerful yellow plaids. Upstairs are the guestrooms and also a delightful, sun-drenched inner courtyard, enhanced by a profusion of potted plants. On warm mornings, breakfast is served here. One of my favorite bedrooms has two tall windows with pretty drapes overlaying lacy curtains, a handsome antique bed, a little sitting area with two darling antique chairs with pretty print cushions, and a private bathroom. The charming ambiance throughout is one of homey, lived-in comfort—nothing fancy or overdone, but just right. If you want to economize, request one of the two bedrooms without a private bathroom. Lois and Terry are marvelous hosts and you soon feel like friends of the family. *Directions:* Exit the A61 at Carcassonne Ouest towards Mazamet. At the fifth roundabout, take the D620 towards Caunes. Follow signs to the *Mairie* (town hall) where parking is often available. L'Ancienne Boulangerie is 20 meters down Rue Saint Genes.

L'ANCIENNE BOULANGERIE
Hosts: Lois & Terry Link
Rue Saint Genes
11160 Caunes-Minervois, France
Tel: 04.68.78.01.32, Fax: none
E-mail: AncienneBoulangerie@compuserve.com
5 rooms, Double: 225F–325F, 2-night min Jul to Sep
No table d'hôte
Open Feb to Dec, Fluent English spoken
Region: Languedoc-Roussillon, Michelin Map 235
www.karenbrown.com/france/lancienneboulangerie.html

The Château des Rochers, a complex of buildings wrapping round a central courtyard of green lawn, is exceptional—it rivals France's finest hotels. Jenny is responsible for the warmth and decor of this outstanding home as well as for the beautiful English garden and dignified landscaping, while Peter is content to settle in as farmer. The entry and ground-floor salon are spectacular—a large, high-mantled fireplace is a magnificent focal point for the furnishings in the beautiful grand salon. Up an elegant staircase is another lovely sitting room and then along the hallway you find the absolutely gorgeous bedchambers. Large, airy, and comfortably furnished with chairs, chests of drawers, armoires, desks, and excellent reading lamps, the rooms and their fully modern bathrooms couldn't be better nor more comfortably furnished. Their decor is refined and elegant, with rich, gorgeous fabrics and beautiful artwork. Thoughtful touches such as coffee makers, sewing kits, evening goodies/snacks, fresh flowers, bathrobes, and slippers are much appreciated. The Alliotts, who hail from England, do not offer table d'hôte but are ready with many local recommendations. *Directions:* From Bayeux take the D972 south towards Balleroy and Saint-Lo. Pass the turnoff to Cerisy La Forêt at the large roundabout at the edge of the forest but continue on the main road signed to Saint-Lo for 3.2 km and turn right to Cerisy La Forêt on D66 (marked D34 on the map). Travel 2.7 km and look for a farm drive with white fencing on the left. The house is set back .8 km off the road.

CHÂTEAU DES ROCHERS   **New**
Hosts: Jenny & Peter Alliott
50680 Cerisy La Forêt, France
Tel & fax: 02.33.56.89.55
5 rooms, Double: 600F–700F
No table d'hôte
Open end of Mar to Nov
Credit cards: VS, Fluent English spoken
Region: Normandy, Michelin Map: 231

Ferme de Launay is an enchanting 18th-century, stone farmhouse draped in ivy and edged by colorful flowers. Inside, the appealing country-cottage ambiance continues. The living room is painted a deep red, setting off to perfection large floral prints and comfortable sofas and chairs grouped around a large open fireplace. Making a stay here especially outstanding is a genuine warmth of welcome, enhanced by a professionalism rarely found in such a small property. This is not surprising—your host is far from an amateur. Jean-Pierre Schweizer, who is Swiss, grew up in the hotel business and has been involved with management of fine hotels since he was a boy. He enjoys entertaining guests and takes great pleasure in making everyone feel at home. Also, he is a superb cook, creating such memorable meals that you will quickly put away any idea of going out to dine. This is a most appealing bed and breakfast—every detail of the decor is perfect. There are three cozy, individually decorated guestrooms, each with pretty wallpaper, beautiful fabrics, top-notch mattresses, quality linens, and excellent bathrooms. *Directions:* Follow N152 east for 9 km from Tours, then turn left in Vouvray onto the D46 towards Vernou. Before Chançay, Ferme de Launay is on your left.

FERME DE LAUNAY (*Gîtes de France*)
Host: Jean-Pierre Schweizer
37210 Chançay, France
Tel & fax: 02.47.52.28.21
3 rooms, Double: 500F–600F
2-night minimum May to Oct
Discount for 3 or more nights
Table d'hôte: 150F per person
Open all year, Fluent English spoken
No smoking house, Children accepted over 15
Region: Loire Valley, Michelin Map 238
www.karenbrown.com/france/fermedelaunay.htm

The Manoir de Ponsay is a superb country farm estate surrounded by rolling pastures, fields of wheat, and pockets of woodlands. As you drive up the winding lane and arrive in front of the stately stone manor, you will be warmly greeted by your charming hosts, Madame and Monsieur de Ponsay. Upon entering their spacious home, you notice an abundance of handsome antiques, old prints, and family portraits. Nothing looks contrived or chosen by a fancy decorator to fit the space—everything looks as if it has been there forever. It has. This lovely home has been passed down through 12 generations, from father to son, since 1644. Madame de Ponsay said with a smile, "I have one child, luckily he's a boy!" A stone staircase spirals up to the bedrooms. Four are extremely large and beautifully decorated in antiques (my favorite, Chambre Fleur, has pale-pink wallpaper setting off pretty pink-and-green floral fabric used on the bedcovers and repeated on the draperies). There are three additional less-expensive bedrooms which are very pleasant—just not as regal in size or decor. If it is an evening when table d'hôte is offered, by all means accept: the meals are outstanding. *Directions:* From the A83 (Nantes-Niort) take exit 6 and go northeast 11 km to Chantonnay. From Chantonnay take the D949b east in the direction of Poitiers. Just a few kilometers beyond Chantonnay, turn left in Saint Mars-des-Prés on a small road towards Puybelliard and follow signs to the Manoir de Ponsay.

MANOIR DE PONSAY
Hosts: Liliane & Marc de Ponsay
Saint Mars-des-Près
85110 Chantonnay, France
Tel: 02.51.46.96.71, Fax: 02.51.46.80.07
E-mail: manoir.de.ponsay@wanadoo.fr
7 rooms, Double: 440F–680F
Table d'hôte: 180F per person, includes wine
Open all year, Credit cards: AX, Good English spoken
Region: Pays de la Loire, Michelin Map 233

When the Lamberts were looking for a home close to Avignon, they fell in love with a charming, 18th-century manor, but it was much larger than they needed for their small family. Happily, Elisabeth's friend, Martine Maret (of La Maison aux Volets Bleus in Venasque), had the perfect solution—open a bed and breakfast. So the Lamberts bought the house and renovated it, making five spacious bedrooms for guests, each with a king-sized bed and a large bathroom. Knickknacks, dolls, and family memorabilia give all the rooms a homey, lived-in ambiance. My favorite guestroom, La Cigale, is especially appealing, with windows looking down to a lovely, secluded pine forest. The heart of the home, the charming kitchen, has a large fireplace on one wall, a multi-colored tile floor, and fragrant sprigs of lavender draped from the open-beamed ceiling, all combining to make this a cozy setting for breakfast. However, breakfast is usually served outside in the delightful walled garden. The Lamberts are extremely gracious, natural hosts who seem to genuinely enjoy guests. They spent five years in the USA and speak excellent English. *Directions:* Take exit 23 (Avignon Nord) from the A7, following signs on D6 to Vedène. Continue on D6 through Saint Saturnin to Jonquerettes. Turn right in the center of the village on D97 and go up the hill. As the road starts down the hill, the entrance to Le Clos des Saumanes is on the left side of the road, opposite a "road narrows" sign.

LE CLOS DES SAUMANES
Hostess: Elisabeth Lambert
519 Chemin de la Garrigue
84470 Châteauneuf de Gadagne, France
Tel: 04.90.22.30.86, Fax: 04.90.22.30.68
E-mail: closaumane@aol.com
5 rooms, Double: 400F–450F, No table d'hôte
Open Easter to Nov (rest of year on request)
Fluent English spoken
Region: Provence, Michelin Map 245

The Château de la Poitevinière and its neighboring lavish châteaux remain as evidence of the decadent lifestyle and grandeur of the French court. Dating back over 200 years, the Château de la Poitevinière is situated 6 kilometers to the north of the medieval village of Chinon. This was a private home until 1985 when it was purchased by Americans who impressively restored the house and incorporated every imaginable modern-day convenience and then sold it to its present owners in 1998. Marie-Christine is delightful and, having lived in the United States for five years, speaks excellent English. The château is furnished with antiques and art that maintain the integrity and ambiance of an 18th-century French château and dramatically and beautifully incorporate mementos of the Pesquets' travels in China, Africa, the United States, and Italy. There are five spacious bedrooms (each with luxurious bathroom) which open onto glorious views over the lovely 12 acres of park and gardens. Canelle, with pastoral views from the bed itself, proves to be the most popular room. Breakfast is served in the sunny dining room. *Directions:* From Chinon or Tours take the D751 to the D16 (in the direction of Huismes), then north 6 km to the D118 left turn—La Poitevinière is noted by a small sign that directs you down a tree-lined drive on the right.

CHÂTEAU DE LA POITEVINIÈRE
Hostess: Marie-Christine Pesquet
37420 Huismes, France
Tel: 02.47.95.58.40, Fax: 02.47.95.43.43
E-mail: pesquet@chateauloire.com
5 rooms, Double: 700F
No table d'hôte, No smoking
Open Apr to Dec, Fluent English spoken
Region: Loire Valley, Michelin Map 232
www.karenbrown.com/france/chateaudelapoiteviniere.html

Saint Paul de Vence, nestled in the green hills above Nice, has always been one of our favorite walled villages, but we had never been able to find a suitable bed and breakfast there. We were delighted, therefore, when a reader wrote in glowing praise of Le Clos de Saint Paul, just a few minutes' drive away. It sounded too good to be true: a beautiful house, spacious gardens, large swimming pool, stylishly-decorated rooms, delicious breakfast, and outstanding hospitality—all at an unbelievably great-value price. Our reader did not exaggerate: Le Clos de Saint Paul is indeed a gem. Hedges and a high wall enwrap the property, giving it an air of seclusion. The home is built in the regional style with thick stuccoed walls, green shutters, and a heavy tiled roof. Mature shade trees dot the lawn and an especially large swimming pool is available for guests' use. The prettily decorated bedrooms are not large, but quite big enough and offer every comfort. My favorite, Les Pivoines, decorated in happy floral fabrics, is a double room with its own terrace opening onto the garden. Breakfast is served each morning in a sunny, glass-enclosed veranda overlooking the garden and the pool. *Directions:* From the A8 take the Cagnes exit (number 47) and follow signs toward Saint Paul de Vence. After passing the roundabout at La Colle sur Loup, go 200 meters and turn right following signs for "Groupe Scolaire Pierre Teisseire." You will see a small sign on your right for Le Clos de Saint Paul.

LE CLOS DE SAINT PAUL
Hostess: Béatrice Ronin Pillet
71, Chemin de la Rouguière
06480 La Colle sur Loup, France
Tel & fax: 04.93.32.56.81
3 rooms, Double: 350F–380F
No table d'hôte
Open all year, 3-night minimum
Very good English spoken
Region: Provence-Riviera, Michelin Map 245

Le Coin Savoyard is located in the heart of Combloux, just across the street from the church. Even without seeing the date of 1819 engraved in the stone above the front door, it is obvious this charming little hotel is quite old. It looks as if it was once a farmhouse, and indeed it was. The home belonged to Colette Astay's grandfather who not only had a farm, but also ran an informal little bar where the locals could have a drink after a day of work. Colette's parents expanded the bar into a restaurant with a few rooms, and now Colette and her husband Philippe have greatly upgraded the property. Although it is still a simple hotel, the bedrooms now are very pretty. All are wood paneled and have matching bedspreads and drapes in pretty Provençal fabrics with a color scheme that varies from room to room. The dining room continues the same country look. It makes no pretense to be decorator-perfect, but rather exudes a refreshing quality of "realness" so often missed when interior designers try to make things too cute. There is a set dinner menu which varies each day, featuring regional specialties and local wines in a very reasonably priced four-course meal. Another bonus is that behind the hotel is a large swimming pool. *Directions:* From Chamonix take A40 west to the Sallanches exit. From Sallanches take N212 south towards Megève. In about 7 km you see a sign for Combloux.

LE COIN SAVOYARD
Hosts: Colette & Philippe Astay
74920 Combloux, France
Tel: 04.50.58.60.27, Fax: 04.50.58.64.44
10 rooms, Double: from 510F
No table d'hôte, restaurant
Open Jun to Sep & Dec to Apr, Credit cards: MC, VS
Some English spoken
Region: Haute Savoie, Michelin Map 244

Usually the places to stay that we suggest are quite old, filled with historical ambiance. Not so with La Rabouillère—it is new. The home was designed by the owner, Jean Marie, who actually built it himself on weekends. There is a story-book quality to this brick-and-timbered bed and breakfast with a steeply pitched roof accentuated by perky gables. You enter into a large family room where guests gather before the open fire in the winter. Antiques abound, and with the beamed ceiling, timber, and exposed brick walls, the mood is certainly old-world. This family/living room is where Martine serves breakfast on chilly mornings, although when the days are balmy guests frequently prefer to eat outside. Martine lovingly decorated each bedroom with Laura-Ashley-type fabrics and antique accent pieces. The rooms are all named after flowers. My favorite, Les Jonquilles, is decorated in soft yellows. All of the bathrooms are spacious and offer special amenities such as built-in hairdryers. In addition to the five bedrooms, there is a two-bedroom apartment. The setting too is superb: a 17-acre wooded estate with a small pond in front. For those who are château-sightseeing, La Rabouillère is right in the heart of the Loire Valley. *Directions:* Go south from Blois on D765 for about 9 km to Cour-Cheverny then take D102 towards Contres. About 6 km beyond Cheverny, turn left following the La Rabouillère signs.

LA RABOUILLÈRE (Gîtes de France)
Hostess: Martine Thimonnier
Chemin de Marçon
41700 Contres, France
Tel: 02.54.79.05.14, Fax: 02.54.79.59.39
5 rooms, Double: 360F–550F, 2-bed apt: 800F
No table d'hôte
Open all year, Credit cards: all major
Some English spoken
Region: Loire Valley, Michelin Map 238
www.karenbrown.com/france/larabouillere.html

Upon Dennis's retirement from the British Diplomatic Service, the Thornleys decided for the first time in their lives to put down roots. They bought a 13th-century watchtower full of character with an extraordinary setting on a slope just below Cordes-sur-Ciel, classified as one of France's most beautiful villages. The Thornleys restored the property, which looks out to a sweeping view of the valley. Capturing the same view is a very large, exceptionally attractive swimming pool. All of the sweetly decorated guestrooms have their own entrance and flowered balcony or patio. Cordes has many restaurants, but for those who prefer to "eat in," there is a summer kitchen with a refrigerator and barbecue where guests may fix a meal. Next to the kitchen is a garden sitting room. For such reasonably priced accommodations, the amenities are outstanding—including large bars of soap that far surpass those often found in deluxe hotels. However, the great merit of this small bed and breakfast is the genuine, unpretentious friendliness of the Thornleys. As Dennis said, they are doing almost what they did for many years in the diplomatic service—just on a more personal level. *Directions:* Upon arrival in lower Cordes, take the cobbled street up the hill at the "Cité" sign. After 400 meters, take the left fork down the hill, marked with two small signs "Le Bouysset" and "Aurifat." Aurifat is signposted on your right, about 200 meters after a hairpin curve.

AURIFAT (Gîtes de France)
Hosts: Patricia & Dennis Thornley
Aurifat, 81170 Cordes-sur-Ciel, France
Tel: 05.63.56.07.03, Fax: none
3 rooms & 2-room suite, Double: 300F
Suite: 550F (4 persons), discount for 7 nights, 3-night min.
No table d'hôte, No children
Open May to Oct, Fluent English spoken
Region: Midi-Pyrenees, Michelin Map 235
www.karenbrown.com/france/aurifat.html

Susanna McGrath, who is Scottish, was looking for a place with character in the Loire Valley where she could open a bed and breakfast. When she discovered the beautiful 15th-century Le Logis du Sacriste, located in the quaint village of Cormery, she bought it in three days. The house is adjacent to, and was originally part of, Cormery's historic abbey. The abbey still forms one wall of Susanna's idyllic enclosed garden where dinner is served on balmy evenings. Susanna has brought her own abundant charm and style to the home. She covered the floors in antique terra-cotta tiles, added a fireplace in the lounge, and draped the windows in ever-so-pretty English fabrics. The renovations added all the needed ingredients for guests' comfort without losing the authentic heritage of the house. A narrow wooden staircase still circles up to charming guestrooms. One of my favorites is a romantic room tucked under the eaves which is decorated with pretty green-and-white plaid fabric. The house is simple but exudes the refinement and good taste of your charming hostess, who is also an exceptional cook and for many years had a successful catering business in London. *Directions:* Take the N12 south from Tours then join the N143 and continue on to Cormery (total of about 22 km from Tours). After crossing over the bridge marking the boundary of Cormery, Rue Alcuin is the third road on the left.

LE LOGIS DU SACRISTE (Gîtes de France)
Hostess: Susanna McGrath
3, Rue Alcuin, 37320 Cormery, France
Tel: 02.47.43.08.23, Fax: 02.47.43.05.48
E-mail: sacriste@creaweb.fr
4 rooms, Double: 310F–350F
Table d'hôte: 150F per person, includes wine
Closed Christmas, Credit cards: MC, VS
Fluent English spoken
Region: Loire Valley, Michelin Map 238
www.karenbrown.com/france/logisdusacriste.html

Renaud Gizardin inherited the Moulin de Marsaguet, a picturesque, 200-year-old stone mill hugging the edge of a romantic little lake, from his grandparents. He lives here with his charming wife, Valerie, their three darling children, several friendly dogs, and a cat (plus a menagerie of other "friends"—horses, ducks, chickens, and cows). There is nothing fancy about the Gizardins' well-managed bed and breakfast, but a sense of gentle goodness permeates their home. When the weather is warm, Valerie serves dinner outside family-style on a picnic table. The hearty meals are prepared totally from ingredients from their property, including the foie gras. The prune liqueur served at the end of the meal is made by Valerie's grandfather. A narrow staircase leads up to the bedrooms. Each is sweetly decorated with excellent taste, and each has a sparkling clean bathroom. Fresh bouquets of flowers and a few family antiques add extra appeal. The bedrooms are simple, but outstanding for the price. The Moulin de Marsaguet is about as far from the bustle of civilization as you can get. Just stretch out under a tree, hike, or row your way to the middle of the lake and watch the wild ducks. *Directions:* From Limoges go south on A20. Take exit 41 and follow signs to Coussac-Bonneval. Don't turn into the village but go straight on D17. Just at the end of town, turn right on D57 in the direction of St. Priest. The Moulin de Marsaguet will be marked on your right. (Don't turn to the village of Marsaguet.)

MOULIN DE MARSAGUET (Gîtes de France)
Hosts: Valerie & Renaud Gizardin
87500 Coussac-BonnevalFrance
Tel & fax: 05.55.75.28.29
3 rooms, Double: 240F
Table d'hôte: 90F per person, includes wine
Open all year (winter by reservation)
Good English spoken
Region: Limousin, Michelin Map 239
www.karenbrown.com/france/moulindemarsaguet.html

Manoir de la Brunie, an intimate, 14th-century home made of pretty honey-tone stone, accented with white shutters, is located just on the outskirts of Le Coux, a small town near the River Dordogne. This bed and breakfast is a real beauty, exuding great warmth and charm. There is a happy mood throughout, and the day we visited, the interior seemed to glow as if the sun were shining, even though it was a rainy day—an effect perhaps achieved by all the warm colors used throughout. Your hostess, Ghislaine, doesn't speak English, but she is so genuinely friendly and eager to please that communication should not be a problem. The lounge and room where guests eat breakfast are attractively decorated, with a comfortable homelike ambiance. Upstairs, the guestrooms are beautifully decorated and have especially glamorous bathrooms. I thought my favorite was Alexandre, with its restful creamy tones and canopy bed, until I saw Chloe, an exceptionally spacious, every-so-pretty room decorated in blue toile fabric. If you are traveling with children, Eric, with its adjoining children's room, would be an ideal choice. *Directions:* From Sarlat, take D57 west to Beynac and continue on D703 toward Bergerac. Soon after D703 bridges the Dordogne, you come to Siorac. At Siorac, go across the bridge then go up the hill to Le Coux. Go through the village, turn left at the first street after the *Mairie* (town hall) and go a little over 1 km. Manoir de la Brunie is signposted on your right.

*MANOIR DE LA BRUNIE   **New***
Hosts: Ghislaine & Marc Orefice
24220 Le Coux et Bigaroque, France
Tel & fax: 05.53.29.61.42
E-mail: marc.orefice@wanadoo.fr
5 rooms, Double: 410F–560F
No table d'hôte
Open all year
Very little English spoken
Region: Dordogne, Michelin Map 233

The Chauveaus are antique dealers who have seasoned their expertise and good taste with a touch of whimsy to create wonderfully imaginative decor and furnishings in their 250-year-old home. Do not expect to see the same antique pieces on a second visit, however, as Monsieur Chauveau is fond of pointing out that all furniture is for sale and therefore subject to change. We stayed in a charming attic room with beautiful exposed support beams and an adjoining immaculate bathroom thoughtfully stocked with ample toiletries and luxurious fluffy towels. Floor-level windows overlook the prettily landscaped swimming pool. The most outstanding bedroom is a corner suite decorated in tones of lavender, green, and yellow with windows (even from the enormous bathroom) looking out over the vineyards. The Chauveaus pay great attention to detail and serve an elegant breakfast complete with gold-trimmed china, silver service, and a white linen tablecloth. Contented appetites are assured after beginning the day with an artful display of exotic fruits, warmed croissants, fresh bread, homemade preserves, rich cheese, and country butter. *Directions:* Cravant les Côteaux is located 8 km east of Chinon. Take D21 through Cravant les Côteaux in the direction of Panzoult. Two km after leaving Cravant, look for a sign advertising Pallus, Bernard Chauveau, and then take the next driveway on the right (the only sign lit at night).

DOMAINE DE PALLUS (Gîtes de France)
Hosts: Barbara & Bernard Chauveau
Pallus, Cravant Les Côteaux
37500 Chinon, France
Tel: 02.47.93.08.94, Fax: 02.47.98.43.00
2 rooms, Double: 500F–550F, 1 suite: 500F–600F
No table d'hôte
Open all year, Fluent English, German spoken by Madame
Region: Loire Valley, Michelin Map 232
www.karenbrown.com/france/domainedepallus.html

Le Haras de Crépon offers a lovely pastoral setting and a convenient base for exploring the D-day landing beaches. M and Mme Pascale Landeau are world-famous for raising champion horses and are understandably proud that "Dream with Me" has held the title of world champion for 1998 and 1999, so for anyone who has a fascination with horses a stay here will be most rewarding. When you enter through the stone gates into the graveled courtyard of this handsome gray-slate manor house, you will be impressed by the grandeur of the home and the beauty of its setting—acres of pastures grazed by regal horses give way to farmland. Each of the five guestrooms is named for a horse, which is then featured in the room. We were able to see a few of the guestrooms at the top of a winding stone turret stair. Bleuet de Crépon is a blue-themed, spacious room overlooking the back garden, identified by a painting hanging over the bed. Two rooms which can connect, Prince de Crépon (shower and bath) and Crépon make for a nice family suite. Colors and style are bright and contemporary: I would have preferred more subdued colors, but the rooms are reasonably sized and bathrooms are modern. A makeshift kitchen with microwave, refrigerator, and stovetop is available for guests' use and on gloomy days the large living room with its television and piano is a welcome gathering spot. *Directions:* From the ring road of Caen, take the D22 northwest in the direction of Creully and after Creully, cross the D12 and travel the D65 for 3 km to Crépon.

LE HARAS DE CRÉPON   New
Hosts: M & Mme Pascale Landeau
Le Clos Mondeville
14480 Crépon, France
Tel: 02.31.21.37.37, Fax: 02.31.21.12.12
5 rooms, Double: 390F–550F
Table d'hôte: 150F per person
Open all year, Credit cards: VS
Good English spoken
Region: Normandy, Michelin Map: 231

Crillon Le Brave, a walled hilltop village, is composed of a pretty, small church and a cluster of weathered stone houses. One of these houses, the Clos Saint-Vincent, has been completely renovated and is now a delightful bed and breakfast. Guests enter through large iron gates into a spacious parking area in front of a typical tan-stone building with brown shutters and tiled roof. A large swimming pool on the terrace captures a sweeping view of the surrounding countryside. There is a very attractive lounge for guests with whitewashed walls, tiled floors, a snug nook with a few comfortable chairs for reading, and a large wooden table for dining. The five bedrooms are all very similar in decor with tiled floors, small table and chairs, and color-coordinated, Provençal-style fabrics used as dust ruffles, chair cushions, and drapes. The feeling is very fresh, uncluttered, and pretty. *Directions:* Carpentras is located 24 km northeast of Avignon. From Carpentras take D974 northeast towards Bédoin then after about 10 km, follow road signs to Crillon Le Brave. As the road climbs the hill towards the old village, you see the sign for Clos Saint-Vincent. Turn right at the sign and continue on a small road for about 200 meters. Turn left and continue up the hill. Clos Saint-Vincent is the second driveway on the left.

CLOS SAINT-VINCENT (Gîtes de France)
Hostess: Françoise Vazquez
Les Vergers
84110 Crillon Le Brave, France
Tel: 04.90.65.93.36, Fax: 04.90.12.81.46
5 rooms, Double: 460F–510F
1 cottage 800F–1000F (4 persons)
Table d'hôte: 150F per person, includes wine
Open all year (groups in winter), Good English spoken
Region: Provence, Michelin Maps 245, 246
www.karenbrown.com/france/clossaintvincent.html

It is not often that you can actually reside in a historical monument, but you can do just that at Le Prieuré Saint Michel. When Anne and Pierre Chahine bought the property, it had been sadly neglected but, happily for the lucky traveler, the complex has been authentically restored and is truly a masterpiece. The granary is now used for various exhibitions and concerts, the giant press where the monks produced the Calvados brandy is still intact, and the lovely little chapel is now an art galley featuring the sketches of one of France's great artists, Edgar Chahine, who just happens to be the father of your congenial host. Equally outstanding are the splendid, meticulously tended gardens. There is an old-fashioned rose garden featuring an incredible variety of fragrant roses from days of yore. In contrast there is the "new" rose garden, the iris garden, the herbal gardens, and on and on. Each is laid out as they would have been in the days of old. Two ponds with ducks and swans complete the idyllic scene. In summer, the grounds are open to the public, but guests are assured of their privacy with their own intimate little garden. Each of the bedrooms is handsomely decorated. *Directions:* Take D916 west from Vimoutiers towards Argentan. Just a few kilometers after leaving Vimoutiers, turn right at the sign for Crouttes. Go through town following signs for Le Prieuré Saint Michel.

LE PRIEURÉ SAINT MICHEL (Gîtes de France)
Hosts: Anne & Pierre Chahine
61120 Crouttes, Vimoutiers, France
Tel: 02.33.39.15.15, Fax: 02.33.36.15.16
E-mail: anne.chahine@wanadoo.fr
3 rooms, Double: 500F–700F
No table d'hôte
Open Apr to Nov, Credit cards: MC, VS
Fluent English spoken
Region: Normandy, Michelin Map 231
www.karenbrown.com/france/leprieuresaintmichel.html

Le Logis du Jerzual, named for the street linking the harbor to the Rance, serves as a convenient base from which to enjoy the charm of the medieval city of Dinan. Housed within walls of a traditional *maison bourgeoise*, this bed and breakfast has its own character and ambiance. Dating from the 15th and 18th centuries, the rooms aren't overly large, but comfortable, and Madame Ronsseray extends a warm welcome. The small house is just up a narrow passage from the main street, set behind its own gate and in a terraced garden. The four guestrooms are staggered on different levels and open onto a small stair. A few of the furnishings looked a bit worn but Madame proudly detailed all her redecorating plans. Breakfast is served inside in either one of two small, cozy rooms—a back room with a beautiful old Breton clock and gorgeous sideboard or the other overlooking the front garden. In warm weather breakfast is offered at tables in the garden. *Note*: The location halfway up a cobbled street requires a lot of walking. On first arrival you can actually drive from the port right up the street amongst the pedestrians and park at the narrow passage to the bed and breakfast. Afterwards, Madame will direct you to a free parking lot for residents (which you are considered as an overnight guest). *Directions*: Follow signs to *Le Port*, cross the old bridge, and continue straight across from the bridge up Rue du Petit Fort, (also referred to as *Le Jerzual*). In spite of the stop sign, this street is allowed for services. Le Logis du Jerzual is signposted on the right.

LE LOGIS DU JERZUAL   **New**
Hostess: Sylvie Ronsseray
25–27, Rue du Petit Fort
22100 Dinan, France
Tel: 02.96.85.46.54, Fax: 02.96.39.46.94
4 rooms, Double 290F–420F
No table d'hôte
Open all year, Credit cards: VS
Good English spoken
Region: Brittany, Michelin Map: 230

Mandy and Terry Murphy decided to move from Britain and open a small hotel or bed and breakfast in either France or Italy. They fell in love with the Domaine du Chatelard, a spectacular 225-acre estate with a 14-bedroom mansion, 3 kitchens, countless fireplaces, swimming pool, tennis court, a vast forest with oak and chestnut trees, and a 20-acre private lake. It had been derelict for many years, so there was a tremendous amount of work to be done, but in April 1999, Mandy and Terry, your gracious hosts, welcomed the first guests into their new "home," a beautiful long, low, stone house draped in ivy and fronted by a meticulous garden courtyard. Within, every detail shows love and caring, and a homelike comfort prevails in the elegant, tasteful furnishings. There are several comfortable lounges, one with a giant television showing programs from around the world (for tranquillity, there are no TVs or phones in the rooms). Each guestroom has its own personality and excellent amenities including superb, firm mattresses. The most stunning feature of this property is a marvelous terrace behind the house that looks down to the picturesque lake below. This is the favorite place for guests to enjoy Mandy's outstanding and beautifully presented dinners. *Directions*: From Angoueléme take D939 south toward Périgueux for about 7 km and exit at Ste. Catherine, taking D101 for 2 km to Dirac. Do not go into Dirac: instead take the D104 toward Puymoyen, After about 3 km turn right, following signs to Chatelard.

DOMAINE DU CHATELARD   **New**
Hosts: Mandy & Terry Murphy
Le Got de Dirac, 16410 Dirac, France
Tel & fax: 05.45.60.29.45
10 rooms, Double: 500F–900F
Table d'hôte at individual tables: 220F per person
Open all year, Oct to Mar with reservation only
Credit cards: all major
Fluent English spoken
Region: Charente, Michelin Map: 233

If you want to experience a bed and breakfast at a simple, real working farm, the characterful Le Temple is a good choice. In days gone by this was the farm of the Templers, the knights of the religious order who went to the crusades, and (if you look carefully) in one wing of the courtyard you can still see the Gothic windows of a 12th-century church. Inside, you do not find decorator-perfect rooms or antique decor, but you do experience genuine country hospitality from Chantal and Michel Le Varlet. After entering from the courtyard, there is a simple parlor where in the evening dinner is served family-style at one large table. Here guests can also read or watch television. During the day the choice place to relax is in the enormous walled garden in the rear. There are four guestrooms reached by a hallway with plastic wallpaper. Although the decor is not outstanding, the rooms are immaculately clean and each has a nice bathroom (and the price is reasonable for those on a budget). Chantal is a very good cook and in the evenings prepares hearty, delicious traditional meals using fresh produce from the farm. *Directions:* Coming from Paris, take the Dormans exit from the A4 and turn right on the RD980 towards Dormans. Stay on this road, and in a few minutes (before you reach Passy Grigny) you see the Gîtes de France sign for Le Temple on your right.

LE TEMPLE (Gîtes de France)
Hosts: Chantal & Michel Le Varlet
Passy Grigny, 51700 Dormans, France
Tel: 03.26.52.90.01, Fax: 03.26.52.18.86
4 rooms, Double: 300F
Table d'hôte: 135F–150F per person
Open all year, Some English spoken
Region: Champagne, Michelin Map 237
www.karenbrown.com/france/letemple.html

The Château d'Ecutigny, set in a serene area of gently rolling hills, is a lovely beige-stone home with turrets and a red-tile roof. However, when Françoise and Patrick Rochet bought the property in 1990, it had been sadly neglected for 150 years. The roof had collapsed, the walls had tumbled in, and sheep were the only guests on the premises—the Rochets had to promise to build a new home for them to complete the sale. The renovation is truly astounding, particularly when you realize that Patrick did all the work himself, except for placing the roof beams. Françoise was also totally involved. In addition to helping with the renovations, she did the interior design and sewed all of the drapes and bedspreads. Today the castle, whose foundation dates to the 12th century, is returned to its former glory, even better than before. Now you have running water, central heating, electricity, and private bathrooms for each of the individually decorated guestrooms (my favorite, Parquet, an enormous corner room with stunning views, has a bathroom as large as a normal bedroom). The castle has dungeons, secret passages, and even a 12th-century kitchen where Patrick sometimes makes bread in the ancient bread oven. *Directions:* From Beaune take the D970 for 20 km through Bligny/Ouche. Just after leaving town, turn left on the D33, signposted Ecutigny. Just at the end of Ecutigny, turn right towards Bessey La Cour and the castle is on your right.

CHÂTEAU D'ECUTIGNY (Gîtes de France)
Hosts: Françoise & Patrick Rochet
Ecutigny, 21360 Bligny-sur-Ouche, France
Tel: 03.80.20.19.14, Fax: 03.80.20.19.15
E-mail: chateau.ecutigny@wanadoo.fr
6 rooms, Double: 500F–700F, Suite: 700F–1,000F
Table d'hôte: 250F per person, includes wine
Open all year, Credit cards: all major
Very good English spoken
Region: Burgundy, Michelin Map: 243
www.karenbrown.com/france/chateaudecutigny.html

Les Patrus, a simple 16th-century farmhouse set in the Champenoise countryside, is conveniently close to Paris by car or train and within an easy drive of Euro Disneyland. Les Patrus's stucco-covered stone buildings form a square, completely enclosing a central grassy courtyard. One of the most popular places in the house is a magnificent dining room dominated by a large fireplace. Here you find five comfortable white sofas and a large dining table that seats up to 15 people. In this welcoming room, furnished with antiques and with large windows, guests gather to eat and share their experiences of the day. Adjacent to the dining room is a bright hall with wooden stairs leading up to a library on the mezzanine. To the right of the library is the Berry suite made up of two bedrooms and a shared bathroom—a perfect setup if traveling with children. My favorite room, the Poitou, looks out over the tiled roofs to rolling fields and a tranquil pond. Mary Ann runs Les Patrus with warmth and efficiency—she has a gift of making her guests feel genuinely at home. An added bonus is her fluent English—not surprising as her father (a Texan) returned to France after World War II to marry his French sweetheart. Les Patrus also has a modern art gallery based on the 17th-century fables of Jean de la Fontaine (Aesop). *Directions:* From the A4, take the Saint Jean/Les Deux Jumeaux exit and head east on D407 and D933 towards Montmirail to the village of La Haute Épine. Turn right towards L'Épine aux Bois. Les Patrus is 500 meters along on your right.

LES PATRUS (*Gîtes de France*)
Hosts: Mary Ann & Marc Royol
02450 L'Épine aux Bois, France
Tel: 03.23.69.85.85, Fax: 03.23.69.98.49
E-mail: les.patrus@wanadoo.fr
3 rooms, Double: 350F–480F, 2 suites: 650F (4 persons)
Table d'hôte: 140F–160F per person, includes wine
Open all year, Credit cards: MC, VS
Fluent English spoken
Region: Champagne, Michelin Map 237

Tucked in the shadow of the church steeple, "La Cure"—once home to the presbytery of the 18th century—offers a tranquil respite in a small Burgundian hamlet. A charming creamstone building with gray-blue shutters at the windows, "La Cure" has second-story windows popping through the pitch of its old tile roof. A heavy, latched old wooden door serves as the entry to this delightful lodging set in a garden of lawn and glorious flowers. Purchased years ago as a family vacation home, it definitely exudes a feeling of home and familiar warmth. An intimate sitting area is a wonderful place to gather with your hosts and other guests for an apéritif before sampling one of the local restaurants. Breakfast is served at a beautiful old wooden table next to the library. Tucked upstairs, the three guestrooms are furnished with comfortable beds and bathrooms are modern. Pretty, traditional fabrics have been chosen for the spreads, but the charm is in the simplicity of the decor—the whitewashed walls, exposed beams, and windows that open up to a bucolic countryside setting with areas of pasture grazed by cattle and fields of wheat. The Renys are a handsome, charming couple who have graciously opened their home to guests. "La Cure" is just 15 miles from the heart of Burgundy, its architecture, and gastronomy. *Directions:* From Beaune take the D910 west toward Bigny-sur-Ouche, then at Bligny, take the D17 toward Arnay-le-Duc. At Foissy, turn left to the church. The house is on the left behind the church.

"LA CURE"
Hosts: Monsieur & Madame Claude Reny
21230 Foissy, France
Tel & fax: 03.80.84.22.92
3 rooms, Double: 400F
No table d'hôte
Open Easter to Nov
Fluent English spoken
Region: Burgundy, Michelin Map 243

Le Domaine de Mestré, a former agricultural estate belonging to the Fontevraud Abbey, dates back to the 12th century. Its origins are even older—stones in the courtyard show traces of an ancient Roman road. You enter through gates into the courtyard. Immediately to your left is a pretty barn which now houses an attractive boutique featuring beautifully packaged soaps and bath oils (sold under the trade name of Martin de Candre). These are manufactured right on the property by three generations of the Dauge family. Because all their products are without any artificial coloring, fragrances, or chemicals, they are very popular—some even exported to the United States. Across the courtyard from the boutique, the 12th-century chapel has been converted into the dining room, attractively decorated with yellow walls and small tables set with yellow linens. The bedrooms are in two separate stone buildings which also face onto the courtyard. Although not deluxe, all of the bedrooms are attractive and most have antique furniture and feature Laura Ashley fabrics. The gracious Dauge family strive to make each guest feel welcome in their home. Rosine prepares lovely meals using ingredients from the estate farm. *Directions:* Take the N152 (Tours to Samur) and cross the river to Montsoreau. From Montsoreau take D947 towards Fontevraud l'Abbaye. Soon after leaving Montsoreau (before reaching the town of Fontevraud l'Abbaye), you see the sign where you turn right for Le Domaine de Mestré.

LE DOMAINE DE MESTRÉ
Hosts: Rosine & Dominique & Marie Amélie Dauge
49590 Fontevraud l'Abbaye, France
Tel: 02.41.51.75.87 or 02.41.51.72.32, Fax: 02.41.51.71.90
E-mail: domaine-de-mestre@wanadoo.fr
12 rooms, Double: 405F
Table d'hôte: 145F per person
Open Apr to Dec 20, open weekends only Mar
Very good English spoken by son-in-law
Region: Loire Valley, Michelin Map 232
www.karenbrown.com/france/ledomainedumestre.html

Located in the sweet village of Fontvieille (just minutes from Les Baux, Saint Remy, and Arles), Mas de la Tour is truly an outstanding find. High stone walls surround the grounds so it is not until you enter the gates that the stunning beauty of the property is revealed—a romantic, picture-perfect 17th-century home with rustic tiled roof and dark-green shutters. The house is surrounded by a gorgeous, perfectly tended garden, and nestled in one corner of the lush, tree-dotted lawn is a splendid swimming pool. Inside there are five large guestrooms, each individually decorated. There is not a hint of commercialism—it truly feels as if you are a lucky guest in a private home. However, behind the scenes every tiny detail for guests' comfort has been well thought out (the bedrooms even have direct-dial telephones). Your charming hostess, Madame Burnet, is no amateur—before opening Mas de la Tour, she owned many large resort hotels. Monique is also a fabulous cook and one of our readers reported that he had the best meal in all of France at her table. *Directions:* As you come into Fontvieille on the D33 from Tarascon, do not turn into the town center, but continue straight ahead. On your right you will pass Hostellerie de la Tour. Soon after, you come to La Tour des Abbés on your right. Opposite La Tour des Abbés, turn left onto Rue de la Tour and look for number 13.

MAS DE LA TOUR
Hostess: Monique Burnet
13, Rue de la Tour
13990 Fontvieille, France
Tel: 04.90.54.76.43, Fax: 04.90.54.76.50
E-mail: m_burnet@clubinternet.fr
5 rooms, Double: 450F–600F
Table d'hôte: 150F per person, includes wine (twice a week)
Open all year, Some English spoken
Region: Provence, Michelin Map 245
www.karenbrown.com/france/masdelatour.html

Since the 15th century the splendid Château de Garrevaques has passed down through the generations in the same family. It was continuously used as the family's home until the charming, effervescent Marie-Christine persuaded her mother to open the château as a bed and breakfast. In fact, the creative Marie-Christine originated the concept (which quickly spread) of owners of beautiful private manors opening their doors and hearts to paying guests. Marie-Christine, a retired purser with Air France, and her husband, Claude Combes, live at the château, where she helps her mother run their successful business. The château is lovingly decorated with heirlooms, and exudes great warmth and genuine hospitality. If you have heard the French are aloof, a visit to Château de Garrevaques will quickly dispel that myth—even the pets are super friendly. After a day of sightseeing, there are both a swimming pool and a tennis court to enjoy. Dinner is a gala event and great fun—filled with tales of the château (ask about the baby born in prison during the revolution who later retrieved his heritage or the faithful gardener who rescued the castle from destruction by the Nazis). *Directions:* From Toulouse take D2/D622 southeast for about 55 km to Revel. Turn northwest on D79 (opposite the police station) for 5 km to Garrevaques.

CHÂTEAU DE GARREVAQUES
Hosts: Marie-Christine Combes & Andrée Barande
81700 Garrevaques, France
Tel: 05.63.75.04.54, Fax: 05.63.70.26.44
E-mail: m.c.Combes@wanadoo.fr
12 rooms, Double: 680F–700F
2 suites (3–5 persons): 1,200F
Table d'hôte: 170F per person, includes wine
Open Mar 15 to Dec (groups in winter), Credit cards: AX, VS
Good English spoken
Region: Tarn, Michelin Map 235
www.karenbrown.com/france/chateaudegarrevaques.html

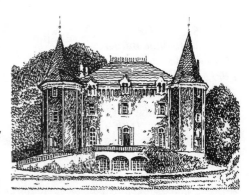

It is a short walk through grassy fields to the sea from this wonderful 17th-century manor house. Francois and Agnes Lemarié are a friendly young couple who, along with their four children, enjoy welcoming bed and breakfast guests to their working farm. A strong sense of the past prevails inside the old stone walls of the Lemariés' home and in the adjoining 15th-century chapel converted to a salon for relaxing and listening to music. The past lives on too in the large stone dovecote in the courtyard. This circular dovecote with hundreds of former pigeon niches provides a unique ambiance for guests to enjoy picnics or light meals. Guest bedrooms are basic, and furnishings vary from very simple to family antiques. Dried-flower bouquets warm the somewhat cool stone rooms. Breakfast is served in the Lemariés' dining room reminiscent of days gone by, with its walk-in stone fireplace and hanging copper kettle, heavy beamed ceiling, and old farm furniture. *Directions:* Géfosse is located approximately 30 km northwest of Bayeux. Take N13 west just past Saint Germain du Pert, exit at Osmansville, then take D514 north towards Grandcamp Maisy. Turn left onto D199A to Géfosse. There are roadside signs for several Chambres d'Hôtes so be sure to follow those marked L'Hermerel. It is the second driveway on the right.

FERME DE L'HERMEREL (Gîtes de France)
Hosts: Agnes & Francois Lemarié
14230 Géfosse
Fontenay, France
Tel & fax: 02.31.22.64.12
4 rooms, Double: 300F
No table d'hôte
Open all year, Good English spoken
Region: Normandy, Michelin Map 231
www.karenbrown.com/france/fermedelhermerel.html

Le Moulin de la Roche sits both beautifully and dramatically beside the rushing river on the edge of the village. You enter through the gate into a carefully tended garden with benches set right above the river—an idyllic place to settle. The building, charmingly covered in ivy and roses, has one-, two-, and three-story sections, with the two-story wing housing the majority of guest accommodation. Rooms are named for their color scheme and although quite snug are clean and comfortable, with their own private bathrooms cleverly incorporated into some nook or cranny, and open onto the sound of the rushing stream. Bathrooms, like the bedrooms, are small but functional. On the first floor, the Blue Room is pretty in blues and whites; on the next floor Yellow is lovely with twin beds in greens and yellows and the Rose Room has one double bed and one twin; on the top floor under the eaves, the Ochre Room is definitely the most spacious. The doorway of the main building takes you into the area that once housed the workings of the mill where you find the breakfast dining area. Off the entry a large comfortable salon is available to guests. On the first floor of the main house is the last room, Green, in pretty fabrics of soft green, rose, and checks. Because it shares the owners' home it does not seem as private or as appealing. *Directions:* From Loches, follow the D764 towards Genillé. When in Genillé follow signs to Montrichard. Just outside the village, turn left on D10 towards Bléré—the Moulin is on the left, signed "Chambre d'Hôte."

LE MOULIN DE LA ROCHE   **New**
Hosts: Josette & Clive Miéville
37460 Genillé, France
Tel: 02.47.59.56.58, Fax: 02.47.59.59.62
E-mail: clive.mieville@wanadoo.fr
5 rooms, Double: 340F
No table d'hôte, Closed Dec 21 to Jan 5
Fluent English spoken
Region: Loire Valley, Michelin Map 238

When the Konings family (whose home was Holland) asked a realtor to find a place for them to retire to in Provence, they expected the search to take many years. Amazingly, the perfect property, a very old stone farmhouse with great potential charm, was found almost immediately, so, even though the timing was a bit sooner than anticipated, they bought the farmhouse and restored it into an absolute dream. The nine guestrooms, four with air conditioning, are in a cluster of weathered stone buildings which form a small courtyard. The name of each room gives a clue as to its original use such as The Old Kitchen, The Hayloft, and The Wine Press. Arja Konings has exquisite taste and each room is decorated using country antiques and Provençal fabrics. Most conveniently, the Konings' son, Gerald (born in the United States), is a talented chef. He oversees the small restaurant which is delightfully appealing with massive beamed ceiling, tiled floor, exposed stone walls, and country-style antique furnishings. The dining room opens onto a terrace overlooking the swimming pool. Another dining room was added for smokers. *Directions:* Gordes is located about 38 km northeast of Avignon. From Gordes, head east on the D2 for about 2 km. Turn right (south) on D156 and in just a few minutes you will see La Ferme de la Huppe on your right.

LA FERME DE LA HUPPE
Hosts: Arja & Gerald Konings
Route D156
84220 Gordes France
Tel: 04.90.72.12.25, Fax: 04.90.72.01.83
E-mail: gerald.konings@wanadoo.fr
9 rooms, Double: 400F–750F
No table d'hôte, restaurant (closed Thursdays)
Open Apr to Dec 20, Credit cards: MC, VS
Fluent English spoken
Region: Provence, Michelin Maps 245, 246
www.karenbrown.com/france/lafermedelahuppe.html

The Moulin de Fresquet is truly a jewel, offering not only the charm of an old mill, but also beautiful antiques and supreme warmth of welcome. The heart of the old stone mill dates back to the 17th century. The millstream still flows right beneath the house—in fact, from several of the guestrooms you can look out the casement windows and watch the gurgling waters. Many places to stay in this price range are pleasant, but lacking in style: not so with Moulin de Fresquet. The family room where guests gather for dinner is filled with beautiful antiques that Gérard inherited from his grandmother. The ambiance is one of rustic beauty with handsome stone walls accented by family portraits and 200-year-old tapestries, heavy beamed ceiling, bouquets of fresh flowers, and a massive stone fireplace. A narrow staircase leads down to the attractive bedrooms which have color coordinated draperies and bedspreads, and French doors opening onto private patios. One of my favorites, Les Meules, is an especially large room with two double beds, windows overlooking the stream, and a door onto the garden. Claude, so pretty with sparkling brown eyes, is a fabulous cook, and dinner, served family-style at one large table, is an event not to be missed. This pleasing old mill is conveniently located for visiting the fascinating town of Rocamadour. *Directions:* From Gramat take N140 south towards Figeac. Just 500 meters after leaving Gramat, take the small lane on the left signposted to Moulin de Fresquet—the mill is on your right.

MOULIN DE FRESQUET (Gîtes de France)
Hosts: Claude & Gérard Ramelot
46500 GramatFrance
Tel & fax: 05.65.38.70.60, Cellphone: 06.08.85.09.21
5 rooms, Double: 310F–410F
Table d'hôte: 115F per person, includes wine
Open Apr to Nov, Some English spoken
Region: Dordogne, Michelin Maps 235, 239
www.karenbrown.com/france/moulindefresquet.html

If you are looking for a tranquil little hideaway while exploring the beautiful area of Provence, the Domaine du Bois Vert is truly a gem. Although the construction is only a few years old, the clever owners, Jean Peter and Véronique Richard, have tastefully achieved the ambiance of an old farmhouse by incorporating a typical rosy-tan stuccoed exterior, light-blue wooden shutters, and a heavy tiled roof. The mood of antiquity continues within where dark-beamed ceilings, tiled floors, dark wooden doors, and white walls enhance a few carefully chosen country-style Provençal pieces of furniture and country-print fabrics. There are three bedrooms, each immaculately tidy and prettily decorated. The bedroom to the back of the house is especially enticing, with windows looking out onto the oak trees. Meals are not served on a regular basis, but Véronique treats guests who stay a week to a dinner featuring typical regional specialties. The swimming pool is a most refreshing bonus. *Directions:* Grans is approximately 40 km southeast of Arles and 6 km from Salon de Provence. From Grans, go south on D19 (signposted to Lançon-Provence). About 1 km after you pass Grans, turn left on a small road where you will see a Gîtes sign. In a few minutes turn left again at another Gîtes sign and take the lane to the Domaine du Bois Vert.

DOMAINE DU BOIS VERT (Gîtes de France)
Hosts: Véronique & Jean Peter Richard
Quartier Montauban
13450 GransFrance
Tel & fax: 04.90.55.82.98
3 rooms, Double: 310F–360F
No table d'hôte
Closed Jan 5 to Mar, Good English spoken
Region: Provence, Michelin Maps 245, 246
www.karenbrown.com/france/domaineduboisvert.htm

Jacqueline and Auguste Bahuaud purchased a handsome manor dating from the mid-1800s and, with great love and labor, meticulously restored the house to its original splendor. Throughout the home everything is fresh, new, and beautifully decorated. The bedrooms are especially outstanding: each has its own personality, each is very inviting. My particular favorite is the Blue Room which has a prime corner location, affording windows on two walls looking out to the rear garden. One of the very nicest aspects of La Croix d'Etain is its setting: the parklike grounds stretch behind the house with terraced lawns shaded by mature trees. A romantic path through the garden leads down to Grez-Neuville, a real gem of a small village nestled on the banks of the Mayenne river. There are many boats along the Mayenne that can be rented by the day or week for exploring the picturesque countryside. Your gracious hosts, Jacqueline and Auguste, warmly open their home and hearts to their guests. *Directions:* From Angers, take N162 north for about 17 km and take a right onto the Grez-Neuville exit. Go into the village and find the old church. As you go down towards the river, you see on your left a beautiful old stone church, and just adjacent to it, the Chambres d'Hôtes sign on the gate of the Bahuauds' home.

LA CROIX D'ETAIN (Gîtes de France)
Hosts: Jacqueline & Auguste Bahuaud
2, Rue de l'Ecluse
49220 Grez-Neuville, France
Tel: 02.41.95.68.49, Fax: 02.41.18.02.72
4 rooms, Double: 380F–480F
Table d'hôte: 150F per person
Open all year, Some English spoken
Region: Loire Valley, Michelin Map 232
www.karenbrown.com/france/lacroixdetain.html

During Brigitte Godon's frequent visits to the Saint Tropez area, she had often admired Le Mazet des Mûres, a lovely 19th-century villa, so when the property came up for sale, she and her husband quickly decided to buy it. The timing was superb as Jean Pierre had retired as a movie director and Brigitte was ready to slow down her career as a movie editor. They renovated the house and restored the gardens and what you see today is a charming villa whose pink façade is laced with vines and accented by violet-colored shutters. A front gate leads into a courtyard shaded by an ancient gnarled oak tree and beautified by colorful flowers. In this secluded courtyard white tables and chairs are set for breakfast and the evening meal (reservations required). Each bedroom, although not large, enjoys a kitchenette where guests can fix themselves a light meal. My favorite (number 2) is a corner room with a double bed with antique wrought-iron headboard and pretty yellow Provençal-print curtains and bedspread. Guests at Le Mazet des Mûres can enjoy utter tranquillity where only the chirping of the cicadas disturbs the quiet—yet be just minutes from the frenzy of the Côte d'Azur's beach resorts. *Directions:* Take RN98 from Saint Maxime towards Saint Tropez. After 4 km turn right at the roundabout, towards Parc de Grimaud Pierres and Vacances. Go about 1 km and turn right on a tiny lane signposted Le Mazet des Mûres.

LE MAZET DES MÛRES
Hosts: Brigitte & Jean Pierre Decourt
Route du Cros d'Entassi
83310 Grimaud, France
Tel & fax: 04.94.56.44.45
5 rooms, Double: 400F–550F
Table d'hôte: 100F per person, includes wine
Open Easter to mid-Oct, Very good English spoken
Region: Côte d'Azur, Michelin Map 245
www.karenbrown.com/france/lemazetdesmures.html

Dana and Robert Ornsteen, your charming American hosts, lived for many years in Paris before purchasing L'Enclos, an enchanting hamlet in the heart of the idyllic Périgord. The complex (once the domain of the Count de Souffron) encloses a courtyard. On one side is the manor, a creamy-beige, two-story home, prettily accented by white shutters. Also facing the courtyard is a cluster of stone cottages, which exude a whimsical, storybook character with their jumble of steep, weathered, interconnecting rooflines and perky gables. Two guestrooms are found in the manor house—the others occupy the hamlet's ivy-laced, yellow-hued stone cottages. The cottages are named for their "past": La Boulangerie still has its bread ovens, La Chapelle occupies the old church, romantic Rose Cottage has thick stone walls, painted furniture, and Provençal fabrics. Two cottages have full kitchens. The gardens are outstanding, with impeccably manicured lawns, weathered stone walls, and gorgeous flowerbeds. A swimming pool nestles in a lush grassy oasis. Everything is absolute perfection, and the price is incredible for such superb quality. You will love it. *Directions:* From Périgueux take D5 east towards Hautefort. At Tourtoirac turn left on D67, cross the bridge, keep right at the Y, and continue for 1.4 km. Turn left into the lane signposted Pragelier, go down the hill and through the gates to L'Enclos.

L'ENCLOS
Hosts: Dana & Robert Ornsteen
Pragelier, 24390 Hautefort, France
Tel: 05.53.51.11.40, Fax: 05.53 50 37 21
US fax: 1.520.441.4503
E-mail: rornsteen@yahoo.com
2 rooms, 7 cottages, Double: 430F–850F
Table d'hôte: 150F per person, includes wine*
*Wednesdays only Jul & Aug
Open May to Oct 15, 2-night minimum
Fluent English spoken, No children under13
Region: Périgord, Michelin Map 233
www.karenbrown.com/france/lenclos.html

In the lovely Périgord region of France, tucked along the banks of a small river, you find the quaint Le Moulin de la Crouzille. This storybook-perfect, vine-covered old mill abounds with character: it is constructed of mellow-toned, honey-colored stone highlighted by casement windows and pretty white shutters. The steeply pitched roof (a jumble of interesting angles) appears even more whimsical with perky little dormer windows peeking out. Stone steps lead up to the front door which opens directly into a homey living room where comfortable chairs and a sofa are grouped around a large open fireplace. To the left of the fireplace, a door opens to a terrace where dinner is served in the summer. There are two bedrooms, each with its own bathroom down the hall. Our favorite is the bedroom with the wonderful painted four-poster bed. The owners, Diana and John Armitage, born in England, now make France their home. Guests are welcomed as friends and dine with the family—Diana is a superb cook and personally prepares the meals. As an added bonus, guests enjoy a swimming pool within a walled garden. *Directions*: From Périgueux take D5 east towards Hautefort. Pass the village of Tourtoirac, go 2.5 km, and then turn left at a small crossroads signposted La Mouney and La Crouzille. Turn right at the first lane (after crossing the bridge) to Le Moulin de la Crouzille. There is no sign as this is a private home.

LE MOULIN DE LA CROUZILLE
Hosts: Diana & John Armitage
Tourtoirac, 24390 Hautefort, France
Tel & fax: 05.53.51.11.94
E-mail: wolsey@wolseylo.demon.co.uk
2 rooms, Double: 700F
Table d'hôte: 200F per person
Closed Christmas, Fluent English spoken
Region: Périgord, Michelin Map 233

The old manor house of Le Petit Pey is set in pretty grounds and tended with care by energetic hostess Annie de Bosredon, a very charming, refined, yet down-to-earth lady who takes great pleasure in opening her home to guests. Le Petit Pey is a regional stone building with windows and French doors framed by white shutters. The oldest part dates from the 1600s, while the newer wing was added in about 1760. Madame de Bosredon's aristocratic drawing room combines comfort with elegance and is filled with valuable antiques, artifacts, and fresh-cut garden roses. Bedrooms are furnished in family antiques, and each has its own personality. The drawing room and bedrooms are actually in a separate wing of the house, so guests are afforded privacy and the luxury of being at home in the lovely salon. There are plenty of historic walled towns in the region as well as the interesting towns of Issigeac and Bergerac. *Directions:* Issigeac is approximately 60 km south of Périgueux via 21 through Bergerac. About 11 km after Bergerac, turn left onto D14 towards Issigeac, then at Issigeac take D21 south towards Castillonnes. Two km later at Monmarvès, look for a sign reading Domaine du Petit Pey and turn into the green gate.

LE PETIT PEY (Gîtes de France)
Hostess: Annie de Bosredon
Monmarvès
24560 Issigeac, France
Tel: 05.53.58.70.61, Fax: none
2 rooms, Double: 320F
No table d'hôte
Open Easter to Oct 10, Good English spoken
Region: Périgord, Michelin Map 235
www.karenbrown.com/france/lepetitpey.html

The Château du Plessis is a lovely, aristocratic country home, truly one of France's most exceptional private châteaux and a personal favorite. Madame Benoist's family has lived here since well before the revolution, but the antiques throughout the home are later acquisitions of her great-great-great-grandfather, as the furnishings original to the house were burned on the front lawn by the revolutionaries in 1793. Furnishings throughout the home are elegant, yet the Benoists establish an atmosphere of homey comfort. Artistic fresh-flower arrangements abound and one can see Madame's cutting garden from the French doors in the salon which open onto the lush grounds. In the evening the large oval table in the dining room provides an opportunity to enjoy the company of other guests and the country-fresh cuisine of Madame Benoist. The Benoists are a handsome couple who take great pride in their home and the welcome they extend to their guests and they are pleased to share the news that their daughter, Valerie, and her family will join their efforts in the year 2000. *Directions:* To reach La Jaille-Yvon travel north of Angers on N162 and at the town of Le Lion d'Angers clock the odometer 11 km farther north to an intersection, Carrefour Fleur de Lys. Turn east and travel 2½ km to La Jaille-Yvon—the Château du Plessis is on its southern edge.

CHÂTEAU DU PLESSIS
Hosts: Simone & Paul Benoist
49990 La Jaille-Yvon, France
Tel: 02.41.95.12.75, Fax: 02.41.95.14.41
E-mail: plessis.anjou@wanadoo.fr
8 rooms, Double: 650F–850F
Table d'hôte: 280F per person
Open Apr to Nov, Credit cards: all major
Very good English spoken
Region: Loire Valley, Michelin Map 232
www.karenbrown.com/france/chateauduplessis.html

The enchanting Château du Guilguiffin is a gorgeous stone manor accented by white shutters, steeply pitched slate roof, perky dormers, and a profusion of chimneys. A circular drive sweeps to the entrance facing onto a lawn enclosed by a circular wall interrupted by 18th-century columns with unique Oriental motifs which make this 1100-acre property a "historic site." The elegant decor is outstanding, with beamed-ceilings, mellow wood paneling, and heirloom antiques. In contrast to the formal parlor, the breakfast room is delightfully casual—a happy room with pretty yellow walls, blue doors, blue-and-white tiles, and a "walk-in" stone fireplace. Guests enjoy breakfast at one large table topped by a gay Provençal-print cloth. The bedrooms are exquisitely furnished with antiques accented by fabric-covered walls and color-coordinating draperies and bedspreads. The garden too is equally stunning. Early spring presents an unbelievable spectacle of 400,000 daffodils followed by thousands of azaleas and rhododendrons. Barbecues are available so guests can grill fresh fish from the local market and enjoy dinner in the parklike grounds. Restaurants are just ten minutes away. What makes a stay here truly special is the genuine hospitality of your host, Philippe Davy (the château has been handed down in his family for over 900 years). Stay at least a week to explore the best of Brittany. *Directions:* From Quimper, go west on D784 towards Audierne. The Château is on the left, 3 km before Landudec.

CHÂTEAU DU GUILGUIFFIN
Host: Philippe Davy
Guilguiffin, 29710 Landudec, France
Tel: 02.98.91.52.11, Fax: 02.98.91.52.52
E-mail: chateau@guilguiffin.com
6 rooms, Double: 650F–800F, Suite: 1100–1300F (3–4 persons)
No table d'hôte, barbecue in garden
Open Apr to Nov 15, Credit cards: AX, VS
Fluent English spoken, Region: Brittany, Michelin Map 230
www.karenbrown.com/france/chateauduguilguiffin.html

The Château de Lascours has a storybook quality, so if you are passionate about castles, this is the place for you. What makes this château really special is that its moat is still intact, making the château appear to be floating on its own little island. The castle dates back to the 12th century when the Counts of Laudun built a small manor on what was probably a Roman ruin. The two-story stone building, softened by ivy, forms a perfect square around an inner courtyard. Towers on three corners are probably the oldest part of the original structure. Fortunately, the château was spared during the French Revolution, and its colorful history has lived on. As you walk in today, nothing much seems to have changed and an aura of past grandeur permeates the air. You wind up a circular staircase made of stone that has worn smooth through the years to the bedrooms, all of which are enormous and have large bathrooms. The decor reflects the château's former grandeur, with furnishings displaying a faded elegance. Being a guest here is like stepping back into the past, although many amenities have been installed for the comfort of guests, including a swimming pool tucked into the woods that surround the moat. *Note:* The Château de Lascours falls more into the category of a bed and breakfast than a hotel, although the owners are usually not on the premises to personally greet you. *Directions:* 25 km northwest of Avignon. From the A9 take exit 22 then N580 toward Bagnols sur Ceze. Just past L'Ardoise, turn left to Laudun and watch for signs to the château.

CHÂTEAU DE LASCOURS
Hosts: Mme & M Jean-Louis Bastouil
30290 Laudun (Gard), France
Tel: 04.66.50.39.61, Fax: 04.66.50.30.08
E-mail: chateau.de.lascours@wanadoo.fr
6 rooms, Double: 550F–600F
No table d'hôte
Open all year, Some English spoken
Region: Provence, Michelin Map 245

Le Bas du Gast is not in the countryside, but is rather a country estate within a city. Once through the massive green wooden gates, you enter a fantasy land of sculpted hedges, wooded parkland, paths leading to English-style gardens, fish ponds, and secluded nooks for dreaming. The years slip away and you feel as if you are living once again in the 18th century. There is a rare authenticity to this château. During the renovation, there was great integrity in preserving the original character of the building. Your gracious host, François Williot (who has the manner and speech of an English lord of the manor), loves his home and can point out to you the perfect symmetry of the formal gardens whose design dates back many centuries, as well as many of the fine architectural features of the house which you might otherwise miss. The furnishings within the home include stunning family heirlooms from the time of Louis XV. Although formality and grandeur prevail in the furnishings, there is also the comfortable, lived-in ambiance of a family home. There is not a hint of stiff formality in your welcome—you are made to feel like a guest of the family. *Directions:* Follow signs to Centre Ville, then Salle Polyvalente. The château is directly across the street from the *Bibliothèque* which is adjacent to the well-marked *Salle Polyvalente.*

LE BAS DU GAST
Hosts: Monsieur & Madame François Charles Williot
6, Rue de la Halle aux Toiles
53000 Laval, France
Tel: 02.43.49.22.79, Fax: 02.43.56.44.71
5 rooms, Double: 770F–870F, Suite: 1,320F
No table d'hôte
Open Feb to Nov, Credit cards: AX
Fluent English spoken, Children welcome
Region: Loire Valley, Michelin Map 232
www.karenbrown.com/france/lebasdugast.html

From the moment you drive through the gates, you will be enchanted by the Manoir Saint-Gilles, a storybook-perfect, 15th-century château accented by manicured lawns, clipped box hedges, and fragrant rose gardens. It is immediately obvious that the owners are perfectionists for everything is tended immaculately. One wing of the house, a charming two-story stone building accented by a tall turret, is totally dedicated to guests. It has an inviting lounge where small tables with colorful Provençal tablecloths are set in front of a massive stone fireplace. The attractively decorated bedrooms are reached by the stone staircase which spirals up the tower. My favorite is room 3, an exceptionally large room with windows capturing a view of the front garden and the wooded park behind. Your gracious hosts, Monsieur and Madame Naux, have a daughter married to an American, and they seem especially to enjoy entertaining guests from abroad. *Note*: No smoking is allowed inside the building. *Directions:* Coming from Angers on the RN147, take D53 marked to Blou and Saint Philbert. Very soon after leaving the highway, D53 goes over the railroad tracks which are hard to see as they cross beneath the road in a low gully. At the first road after crossing the tracks, turn left at the dead end sign, then turn left again at the first road with the second dead end sign. Go about 300 meters and turn right at the first small lane (third dead end sign). You will see the manor with its white gate at the road's end.

MANOIR SAINT-GILLES (*Gîtes de France*)
Hosts: Monsieur & Madame Naux
49160 Longué, France
Tel: 02.41.38.77.45, Fax: 02.41.52.67.82
E-mail: CMCNAUX@aol.com
4 rooms, Double: 450F–750F, 2-night minimum
No table d'hôte
Open Apr to Nov, No English spoken
Region: Loire Valley, Michelin Map 232
www.karenbrown.com/france/manoirsaintgilles.html

From the moment you drive through the gates, you will be enchanted by the Manoir Saint-Gilles, a storybook-perfect, 15th-century château accented by manicured lawns, clipped box hedges, and fragrant rose gardens. It is immediately obvious that the owners are perfectionists for everything is tended immaculately. One wing of the house, a charming two-story stone building accented by a tall turret, is totally dedicated to guests. It has an inviting lounge where small tables with colorful Provençal tablecloths are set in front of a massive stone fireplace. The attractively decorated bedrooms are reached by the stone staircase which spirals up the tower. My favorite is room 3, an exceptionally large room with windows capturing a view of the front garden and the wooded park behind. Your gracious hosts, Monsieur and Madame Naux, have a daughter married to an American, and they seem especially to enjoy entertaining guests from abroad. *Note*: No smoking is allowed inside the building. *Directions:* Coming from Angers on the RN147, take D53 marked to Blou and Saint Philbert. Very soon after leaving the highway, D53 goes over the railroad tracks which are hard to see as they cross beneath the road in a low gully. At the first road after crossing the tracks, turn left at the dead end sign, then turn left again at the first road with the second dead end sign. Go about 300 meters and turn right at the first small lane (third dead end sign). You will see the manor with its white gate at the road's end.

MANOIR SAINT-GILLES (*Gîtes de France*)
Hosts: Monsieur & Madame Naux
49160 Longué, France
Tel: 02.41.38.77.45, Fax: 02.41.52.67.82
E-mail: cmcnaux@aol.com
4 rooms, Double: 450F–750F, 2-night minimum
No table d'hôte
Open Apr to Nov, No English spoken
Region: Loire Valley, Michelin Map 232
www.karenbrown.com/france/manoirsaintgilles.html

Three hundred meters from Brittany's northern coastline, Madame Sillard's historic home is the former residence of author Ernest Renan. Set in wooded grounds, this small manor house is furnished in lovely country antiques and offers bed and breakfast accommodation to fortunate travelers. A lace-curtained front door leads into the entry hall which is warmly decorated with an antique armoire, bookcase, and dried-flower arrangements. Madame Sillard is a charming, well-traveled hostess who has spent extended periods of time in the United States, thus speaks very good English. Her guest bedrooms are decorated with pretty fabrics and fresh-flower bouquets, while furnishings are a tasteful mix of antiques and some more contemporary pieces. If you are on a budget, request the bedroom without a private bathroom. Breakfast is served at a long wooden table in the country-elegant drawing room where two tabby cats often share the seat of a tapestry chair. *Directions:* Louannec is located approximately 70 km northwest of Saint Brieuc, 40 km northwest of Guingamp. From Lannion (30 km northwest of Guingamp), take D788 north in the direction of Perros Guirec. After 7 km, turn right onto D6 to Louannec. Just before town, there will be a sign indicating Chambres d'Hôtes up a small lane to the right. A driveway on the left leads to Madame's pretty house set back behind a garden.

DEMEURE DE ROSMAPAMON
Hostess: Madame A. Sillard
Louannec
22700 Perros-Guirec, France
Tel: 02.96.23.00.87, Fax: none
4 rooms, Double: 385F, Suite: 420F–470F
No table d'hôte
Open May to Oct, Credit cards: VS
Very good English spoken
Region: Brittany, Michelin Map 230

In its prime, the Château Unang was undoubtedly one of the showplaces of Provence. Today the formal gardens show a genteel neglect and the gorgeous château reflects a faded elegance, but the fairy-tale quality of this 18th-century château remains undimmed. Iron gates open to the inner courtyard, overlooked by the handsome beige-stucco building whose exterior is softened by ivy and whose windows are accented by white wooden shutters. The château fronts onto a gravel terrace with steps leading down to a lower terrace with a garden of clipped hedges forming an intricate design. More steps go down to an even lower level where the vineyards hug the edge of an idyllically positioned swimming pool. The guestrooms are found up a flight of stone steps from the reception hall. Furnished with antiques, the bedrooms are decorated in a homey, comfortable style. My favorite room, Marquessa, has a splendid view of the vineyards. Marie Lefer is your gracious young hostess—Château Unang is her family home. She is in charge of the bed and breakfast while her brother oversees the vineyards and production of the family's wines. *Directions:* From the A7 (Orange to Aix en Provence) take the Avignon North exit. Follow signs to Carpentras then take D4 for 6 km towards Venasque, turning left on D5 to Malemort du Comtat. From Malemort take D5 towards Méthamis. After 1 km there is a small sign on the right leading to Château Unang.

CHÂTEAU UNANG (Gîtes de France)
Hostess: Marie Lefer
84570 Malemort, France
Tel: 04.90.69.71.06, Fax: 04.90.69.92.85
4 rooms, Double: 700F, Suite (Jul & Aug only): 950F
Table d'hôte: 180F per person, includes wine
Open all year, Credit cards: MC, VS
Good English spoken
Region: Provence, Michelin Map 245
www.karenbrown.com/france/chateauunang.html

We received a warm welcome at Monsieur and Madame Bouteillers' charming half-timbered farmhouse where they have made their home for over 40 years. Monsieur explained that he was originally a city boy from Rouen, but always wanted to be a farmer. He has achieved his dream in this pastoral setting where he and his wife have raised seven children and now boast thirteen grandchildren. Madame's table d'hôte dinners always include regional specialties such as creamed chicken, duck with peach sauce, and, of course, one of several varieties of homemade apple tarts. These friendly meals are served in the light and cheerful entry salon with its long table decorated with a wildflower bouquet in an earthenware jug. An antique sideboard and old stone mantel displaying candlesticks and a pewter jug add to the country ambiance. The Bouteillers' two guestrooms are clean and well equipped with simple decor and furnishings, including wooden beds and armoires. *Directions:* Martainville is located approximately 58 km southwest from Rouen via A13 to the Beuzeville exit. In Beuzeville, turn left at the traffic light at the church. Follow signs for the town of Epaignes via route D27. Approximately 6 km later you see a Chambres d'Hôtes sign directing you to turn right. A driveway on the left then leads you to the Bouteillers' low, half-timbered farmhouse.

CHEZ BOUTEILLER (Gîtes de France)
Hosts: Monsieur & Madame Jacques Bouteiller
Martainville
27210 Beuzeville, France
Tel: 02.32.57.82.23, Fax: 02.32.42.21.83
E-mail: annetteb@club-internet.fr
2 rooms, Double: 220F
Table d'hôte: 90F per person
Open all year, Some English spoken by Monsieur
Region: Normandy, Michelin Map 231
www.karenbrown.com/france/chezbouteiller.html

Your charming hosts at La Lumière, Beth and Peter Miller, are English. They moved to France when Peter took early retirement from IBM and purchased a piece of land surrounded by vineyards, fruit trees, and fields of fragrant lavender in one of Provence's most idyllic regions. It took several years to get permission to build, but the struggle was definitely worthwhile. Today they have a charming, blue-shuttered, Provençal-style home nestled in a wooded glen of pines and olive trees, with a beautiful small swimming pool reached by a shaded garden path. They offer one guest suite which includes a prettily decorated sitting room with floral curtains and a small, well-equipped kitchen corner for making tea, coffee or a picnic. An open wooden staircase leads up from the sitting room to the sleeping loft and its king-sized bed. The suite has its own entrance opening onto a flagstone terrace with table and chairs shaded by a parasol. Beth has a great flair for decorating and her home is truly a small gem. She is trained as a chef and organizes wine-appreciation and cooking classes. *Directions*: Take D938 from Vaison La Romaine towards Nyons for about 5 km and turn right on D46 to Puymeras, then take D205 to Mérindol les Oliviers. After La Gloriette restaurant, turn right on CR10, go 650 meters, and La Lumière is on the right in a wooded garden.

LA LUMIÈRE (Gîtes de France)
Hosts: Beth & Peter Miller
Quartier Les Grand Vignes
26170 Mérindol Les Oliviers, France
Tel: 04.75.28.78.12, Fax: 04.75.28.90.11
1 suite, Double: 350F
Table d'hôte: 135F per person, includes wine
Open mid-Apr to mid-Oct, Fluent English spoken
Children over 4 accepted
Region: Provence, Michelin Map 245
www.karenbrown.com/france/lalumiere.html

Le Balcon de Rosine is truly one of Provence's gems. When Jean Bouchet purchased the property over 30 years ago, it was a working farm. Olive trees still dot the steep incline below the shelf where the characterful 18th-century stone home stands, but the farming is now left to the Bouchets' son, for Jean is an artist. His wife, Jacqueline, offers guests a choice of two accommodations, each with its own entrance. The suite located in the main house is very nice, but my favorite is truly spectacular, occupying one end of the stone farm building where Jean has his art studio. This accommodation is like a doll's house: it has a little parlor decorated with pretty blue-and-white Provençal fabric, a small kitchen where the blue-and-white color scheme is repeated in the pottery, and a beamed-ceilinged bedroom with thick whitewashed walls, twin beds, an antique desk, and pink-and-white-striped draperies. Best of all, this suite has its own private, balcony-like terrace beneath which Provence is spread before you—a panorama of vineyards and distant hill towns, and, beyond, row upon row of mountains. If you want a romantic hideaway, this is one of the best in France—and the price is incredible for the value received. *Directions:* Take D938 from Vaison La Romaine towards Nyons for about 5 km and turn right on D46 to Puymeras, then take D205 to Mérindol les Oliviers. Go through town and take the D147 towards Propiac. Le Balcon de Rosine is on your right after 1km.

LE BALCON DE ROSINE (Gîtes de France)
Hosts: Jacqueline & Jean Bouchet
Route de Propiac
26170 Mérindol: Les Oliviers, France
Tel & fax: 04.75.28.71.18
2 rooms, Double: 300F–350F
No table d'hôte
Closed Aug, Good English spoken
Region: Provence, Michelin Map 245
www.karenbrown.com/france/lebalconderosine.html

When the Schlumbergers bought Les Grand' Vignes over 30 years ago, it consisted of two derelict 19th-century farmhouses. François Schlumberger, a talented architect, has done a superb job of renovation, resulting in one charming stone farmhouse accented by brown shutters. Your delightful hostess, Chantal Schlumberger, is a real professional, being one of the first to open her home to guests over 16 years ago. She offers two immaculate, simply decorated guestrooms, one of which is a studio with kitchenette. Chantal also rents one part of the house by the week which accommodates four people. In the garden there is a large swimming pool which guests may use. Also in the garden a kitchen with a refrigerator, barbecue grill, and dinnerware are thoughtfully provided— frequently guests fix themselves a light dinner here. However, the most outstanding feature of Les Grand' Vignes is its stunning setting on a hilltop, dotted with olive trees and fragrant with the scent of lavender. From the terrace where breakfast is served there is an unforgettable, panoramic view and a vineyard so close you can touch the grapes as you sip your morning coffee. *Directions*: Take D938 from Vaison La Romaine towards Nyons for about 5 km and turn right on D46 to Puymeras, then take D205 to Mérindol les Oliviers. Soon after La Gloriette restaurant, turn right on D147—Route de Mollans. The house is the first on the right.

LES GRAND' VIGNES (Gîtes de France)
Hostess: Chantal Schlumberger
Quartier Les Grand Vignes
26170 Mérindol Les Oliviers, France
Tel & fax: 04.75.28.70.22
2 rooms, Double: 300F–350F
No table d'hôte
Open all year, Well behaved children accepted
Good English spoken
Region: Provence, Michelin Map 245
www.karenbrown.com/france/lesgrandvignes.html

The 18th-century Manoir de Clénord is a handsome manor in the heart of the Loire Valley, ideally situated for exploring the rich selection of châteaux in the region. The interior exudes an ambiance of lived-in comfort with handsome family heirlooms used throughout. The dining room—located in the oldest wing of the house—is especially appealing. It has a beamed ceiling, a huge fireplace, and, in the center of the room, a fabulous trestle table, mellowed with the patina of age, where guests sit down family-style for delicious meals. A wooden staircase leads to the guestrooms, each individual in decor like in a private home. Quality wall-coverings color-coordinate with fabrics used on the drapes and beds. The suites are especially elegant. If you are on a tight budget, there is one lovely little room (barely big enough for a double bed) that offers a real bargain. In addition to the manicured formal gardens and expansive surrounding forest, guests can enjoy a large, beautiful swimming pool and tennis court. The owners, Christian Renauld and his fiancée Sylvie Galeraud, are warm, gracious hosts. *Directions:* From Blois go south 10 km on D765 towards Cheverny and Romorantin. At Clénord, turn left at the sign for the Manoir de Clénord. The entrance is signposted on your left.

MANOIR DE CLÉNORD (*Gîtes de France*)
Owner: Christian Renauld
Route de Clénord
41250 Mont Près Chambord, France
Tel: 02.54.70.41.62, Fax: 02.54.70.33.99
E-mail: sg@clenord.com or
 manoir.de.clenord@wanadoo.fr
4 rooms, Double: 400F–700F, 2 Suites: 850F–1,200F
Table d'hôte: 200F per person, includes wine
Open Apr to Nov, Credit cards: all major
Very good English spoken
Region: Loire Valley, Michelin Map 238
www.karenbrown.com/france/manoirdeclenord.html

The Château de Montmaur is a designated historic monument dating from the 14th century. Found in a small village surrounded by tree-covered hills and mountains, the castle is built on a grand scale, with thick stone walls and two great halls. Authentic wood floors, fresco paintings, and huge fireplaces all testify to the castle's colorful past as a fortress, a royal castle, and even a headquarters for resistance fighters during World War II. The Laurens family are dedicated to breathing life into their historic home and have opened the large halls to public tours, weddings, classical music concerts, receptions, and parties. Parts of the castle are still being restored and three intimate suites have been completed for bed and breakfast guests. The rooms are prettily decorated with elegant fabrics and wallpapers and each has a private shower and WC as well as an independent entrance. Breakfast is served in the Laurens's charming salon/dining room which has a beamed ceiling and a lovely stone fireplace and is decorated with country antiques and fresh-flower bouquets. *Directions:* From Genoble take N75 south to Serres where you take N94 east in the direction of Gap. Go through Veynes and in about 4 km turn left following signs for Montmaur: the castle gate is clearly marked at the entry to the village.

CHÂTEAU DE MONTMAUR (Gîtes de France)
Hosts: Elyse & Raymond Laurens
Montmaur
05400 VeynesFrance
Tel & fax: 04.92.58.11.42
3 suites, Double: 450F
No table d'hôte
Open Apr to Nov, No English spoken
Region: French Alps, Michelin Map 245

In Montrésor, one of the most charming villages in France, where narrow, cobbled streets are dramatically shadowed by its castle, the De Laddersous family has transformed an abandoned mill into a lovely home and bed and breakfast. Le Moulin, a handsome old stone building, sits on peaceful acreage at the water's edge just on the outskirts of town. The living room, on the ground floor, is open and spacious, decorated in rich colors of orange, green, and yellow, with sofas and chairs set round a large open fireplace. I love the roar of crashing water—like many people, I find it soothing—but here at Le Moulin you can not only hear it but also watch it cascade spectacularly. The De Laddersouses have cleverly cut into the tiled floor and exposed the rushing water below through big sheets of glass. Climb the stairs off the salon to the four guestrooms, which comprise the four corners of the building. As yet unnamed, they are referred to by color scheme. Two of the four, a very pretty back corner room with twin beds and two windows, and a front corner room with queen bed, feature greens and yellows. Another twin-bedded room with a side view, extra trundle bed, and lovely bathroom is decorated in blue and white, as is the second lovely queen-bedded room. Downstairs, the floor is handsome with exposed tile while upstairs the hallway is of a straw weave. *Directions:* Montrésor is located 17 km from Loches. In Montrésor follow direction of Chemille sur Indrois on the left side of the village.

LE MOULIN DE MONTRÉSOR   **New**
Hosts: Sophie & Alain Willems De Laddersous
37460 Montrésor, France
Tel: 02.47.92.68.20, Fax: 02.47.92.74.61
4 rooms, Double: 290F – 340F
No table d'hôte
Open all year
Very good English spoken
Region: Loire Valley, Michelin Map: 238

La Varinière is an exceptionally lovely and remarkably low-priced bed and breakfast ideally located near the Normandy beaches. This pretty bourgeois home, set in beautiful rolling green countryside, has been lovingly restored by Pippa and David Edney who used to own a successful restaurant in their native England. From the moment you arrive, you cannot help noticing that everything is impeccably kept, from the tidy gardens to the polished furniture and sparkling windows. David and Pippa completely renovated La Varinière, created the lovely garden, wallpapered all the bedrooms, put in bathrooms, sewed drapes, and slipcovered chairs. Downstairs is a riot of bold, happy colors: the entrance hall is bright blue, the parlor raspberry pink, and the dining room exuberant yellow. These colorful rooms look lovely with their coordinating fabrics. In the spacious guestrooms pretty wallpaper, attractive antique beds, and fresh flowers create a most appealing ambiance. The Edneys do not do evening meals but they have thoughtfully provided a refrigerator where guests can store their own drinks or evening picnic supplies. *Directions:* From Caen take the N84 towards Mont Saint Michel and Rennes. After about 18 km take exit No. 45 (Monts-en-Bessin), turn right on to D92 and head towards Monts-en-Bessin. At the crossroads continue straight over and down the hill, take the first right after the church, and La Varinière is the second house on the left.

LA VARINIÈRE   (Gîtes de France)
Hosts: Pippa & David Edney
La Vallée
14310 Monts-en-Bessin, France
Tel: 02.31.77.44.73, Fax: 02.31.77.11.72
5 rooms, Double: 330F
No table d'hôte
Closed Christmas, Fluent English spoken
Region: Normandy, Michelin Map 231
www.karenbrown.com/france/lavariniere.html

When on holiday in France, Marjorie and Brian Aylett (who are English) bought Le Presbytère on a whim. In a matter of three days they were the owners of a magnificent 15th-century rectory next to a picturesque 11th-century village church. There was no plumbing, no water, barely any electricity—only potential. Their transformation is now complete and today their lovely home is warmly furnished with comfortable antiques. There are three spacious bedrooms, each decorated in excellent taste with loving attention to detail. The bathrooms are color-coordinated, beautifully tiled, and enjoy the fluffiest of towels and several large bars of soap. The views from the property are wonderful—uninterrupted fields bordered by trees creating a patchwork of pastoral delight. Like the home, the gardens are now an oasis filled with beautiful flowers, green lawns, and patches of shade trees where benches have been strategically placed in quiet nooks. Marjorie even has her own vegetable garden where she grows produce for the evening meals. Be sure to request the table d'hôte—Marjorie is an excellent cook. Le Presbytère is truly perfection. You could pay twice the price and not experience the charm and quality of this delightful bed and breakfast. *Directions:* Heading south from Paris on A6, take the Bierre les Semur/Saulieu exit onto D980 towards Saulieu. In Saulieu take the D26 for 10 km to La Motte Ternant. Le Presbytère is at the high point of the village just right of the church.

LE PRESBYTÈRE
Hosts: Marjorie & Brian Aylett
La Motte Ternant, 21210 Saulieu, France
Tel: 03.80.84.34.85, Fax: 03.80.84.35.32
3 rooms, Double: 370F–400F (2-night minimum)
Table d'hôte: 130F per person, includes wine
Open all year, Fluent English spoken
No smoking, not suitable for children
Region: Côte d'Or, Michelin Map 243
www.karenbrown.com/france/lepresbytere.html

The Château de la Grande Noë is truly a gem—the idyllic setting, the superb decor, and the genuine warmth of welcome are just what you've always dreamed of finding. The castle, dating back to medieval times, has been in the same family since 1393. You enter through stately gates into a manicured front garden overlooked by the handsome two-story château with intricate brick trim decorating the windows, a steep, gray-slate roof punctuated with gabled windows, and a profusion of tall chimneys. Behind the château horses frolic in the meadow. As you walk up the steps into the reception hall, you feel you have entered into the exquisite home of a friend. Throughout there are beautiful draperies, family portraits, English-style slipcovered sofas, and heirloom antiques. A staircase leads to the guestrooms. All are lovely but my favorite of the three is a large room decorated in tones of pale peach, soft green, and yellow. Pascale de Longcamp is a woman of amazing talents: not only did she decorate the rooms, sew all the drapes, make the bedspreads, and wallpaper the rooms, but she also tiled the bathrooms herself. The most exquisite room in the house is the gorgeous 18th-century oak-paneled dining room, where breakfast is served. *Directions:* Take N12 from Paris towards Alençon. At Carrefour/Saint Anne go south on D918 towards Longny au Perche for 4.5 km then turn left towards Moulicent. The château is on your right in less than 1 km.

CHÂTEAU DE LA GRANDE NOË (Gîtes de France)
Hosts: Pascale & Jacques de Longcamp
61290 Moulicent, France
Tel: 02.33.73.63.30, Fax: 02.33.83.62.92
E-mail: grandenoe@wanadoo.fr
3 rooms, Double: 550F–650F
No table d'hôte
Open Easter to Dec (winter by reservation), Good English spoken
Region: Normandy, Michelin Map 231
www.karenbrown.com/france/chateaudelagrandenoe.html

I had seen photographs of the Château de Colliers, a handsome two-story, buff-colored château with white trim and gray mansard roof, but upon arrival I was in for a wonderful surprise—I had not realized that the château is perched on a terrace overlooking the River Loire. What bliss in the morning to open wide the casement windows, hear the birds sing, and see the river flow by below. A path just below the terrace following the river's edge is perfect for those who like to start the day with an early-morning stroll or jog. The château once belonged to the Marquis of Vaudreuil (Governor of Louisiana and French Canada until 1779). It has been in the same family since that time and thus the furnishings are authentic antiques—nothing contrived in a decorator-perfect way, just old-fashioned comfort. Family portraits adorn many of the walls—it is fun to ask just who they are. Each of the bedrooms is unique in decor, each filled with antiques. No dinner is offered but there are two very good restaurants nearby. There is a small raised swimming pool at the front of the château. *Directions:* From Blois, cross the Loire and take D951 northeast towards Orleans. Before reaching the town of Muides-sur-Loire, you see the château on your left.

CHÂTEAU DE COLLIERS (Gîtes de France)
Hosts: Marie-France & Christian de Gelis
41500 Muides-sur-Loire,France
Tel: 02.54.87.50.75, Fax: 02.54.87.03.64
E-mail: chcolliers@aol.com
5 rooms, Double: 600F–750F, Suite: 750F–1,000F
No table d'hôte
Open all year (winter by reservation)
Credit cards: MC, VS, Very good English spoken
Region: Loire Valley, Michelin Map 238
www.karenbrown.com/france/chateaudecolliers.html

The Manoir de Montflambert, a 17th-century manor house hugging the edge of the forest of Reims, fronts onto a simple farmhouse courtyard. It is only after entering the home that one of its nicest aspects is revealed—behind the house is a large walled garden with a wide expanse of lawn bordered by carefully manicured beds of flowers. This grassy area stretches out to a quiet pond in a wooded glen. Inside, both the dining room and parlor take advantage of the garden view. The dining room is especially attractive, dominated by a large fireplace and handsome dark paneling which, appropriately for the Champagne region, is banded by a design of intricately carved grapes. A graceful 350-year-old staircase of polished wood winds up from the entry hall to the bedrooms, each with walls covered in a corduroy-like velour of a different hue. *Directions:* From the A4 (Paris to Reims) take the Château Thierry/Soissons exit and continue east on N3 to Épernay. From Épernay, cross the river and take D1 east towards Ay and Mareuil where you take the turnoff north to Mutigny. The Manoir de Montflambert is signposted with a Chambres d'Hôtes sign and also the name Rampacek.

MANOIR DE MONTFLAMBERT (Gîtes de France)
Hostess: Renée Rampacek
51160 Mutigny, Marne,France
Tel: 03.26.52.33.21, Fax: 03.26.59.71.08
5 rooms, Double: 450F–650F, 2 suites: 660F–900F
Open Mar 15 to Nov 15
Credit cards: MC, VS
Very little English spoken
Region: Champagne, Michelin Map 237
www.karenbrown.com/france/manoirdemontflambert.html

The Château des Ormeaux, a spectacular, cream-stone castle nestled on the hills above the Loire, reflects the energy, creativity, and insight of four remarkable partners who restored this long-abandoned château to a new life as a luxurious bed and breakfast, while lavishing detail to achieve the home of their dreams. Off the handsome entry the salon is set with comfortable sofas and chairs round a wood-burning fire. Continuing on, the dining room is gorgeous in blues and golds, with a lovely cabinet displaying a wealth of silver and a dramatic, deep-red chair which brings out the reds in the wonderful Oriental carpets. Climb the elegant staircase to the bedchambers, each named for a French composer. On the second floor are three spectacular rooms. At the front, each enjoying a sitting area in the turret round, are Lully, in pretty colors of red and gold, and Couperin, a dramatic room in black and gold contrasting with the blues and creams of the bathroom. At the back, Rameau is a lovely room richly painted in warm yellow with complementing green and rose. On the third floor, Ravel is the smallest guestroom, but quite intimate under the eaves, and both Debussy, in lovely rose and cream, and Poulenc, with its display of blue-and-cream checks on plaids, enjoy the turret round. Endless trails, tennis courts, a gorgeous pool, and wonderful table d'hôte dinners make a stay here an absolute delight. *Directions:* From Tours travel east on the RN152. At Vouvray take the D1 towards Noizay—the château is just east of Noizay at La Bardouillère.

CHÂTEAU DES ORMEAUX   **New**
Owner: Xavier Merle
Hosts: Xavier, Philippe, Emanuel & Serge
Route de Noizay, Nazelles
37350 Amboise, France
Tel: 02.47.23.26.51, Fax: 02.47.23.19.31
E-mail: chateaudesormeaux@wanadoo.fr
6 rooms, Double: 550F & 650F
Table d'hôte: 250F, includes wine
Open all year, Very good English spoken
Region: Loire Valley, Michelin Map 238

Madame Gourlaouen's property enjoys a tranquil location near the spectacular coastline and beaches of southern Brittany and the artist community of Pont Aven. This picturesque port town is the former home of many French impressionist painters, as well as Paul Gauguin. Madame Gourlaouen is a young, capable hostess who offers bed and breakfast as well as apartment accommodation in her pretty stone farmhouse. Dating from 1730, the long, low house is built from the golden-hued stones that are typical of the Concarneau, Pont Aven region. An independent entrance leads to the guest bedrooms which are furnished with antique reproductions. Rooms are small but charming and all have private WC and shower—a great bargain for the money. The intimate breakfast room is full of charm with a low, beamed ceiling, old stone hearth, country antiques, and fresh garden flowers. *Directions:* Nevez is located approximately 30 km southeast of Quimper. Leave the town of Pont Aven on D70 towards Concarneau, turning left just outside town following signs to Nevez. In the village of Nevez, continue past the church, then take the left fork in the road onto D77 towards Port Manech. After about 4 km, just before entering Port Manech, look for a Chambres d'Hôtes sign directing you to turn right. Continue following signs, turning at the first left, and you will arrive at this sunny farmhouse 300 meters from the sea and rocky promontory.

CHEZ GOURLAOUEN (*Gîtes de France*)
Hostess: Yveline Gourlaouen
Port Manech, 29920 Nevez, France
Tel: 02.98.06.83.82, Fax: none
6 rooms, Double: 250F
No table d'hôte
Open mid-Mar to mid-Nov
Some English spoken
Region: Brittany, Michelin Map 230
www.karenbrown.com/france/chezgourlaouen.html

The Chez Langlais is a hidden jewel. From the outside, the house looks nondescript and the neighborhood rather ho-hum, but once you enter through the white side gate into the back garden, the scene is magically changed. You are surrounded by a garden filled with flowers and fruit trees and the property, which looks small from the front, stretches all the way out to a tiny river. The home itself takes on a whole new dimension: seen from the back, the white house with steeply sloping roof and gables is as cozy as can be. White tables and chairs are set out under the trees, an oasis where guests gather after a day of busy sightseeing to relax and share their experiences. The living room, with its beamed ceiling and exposed stone walls, offers a cozy retreat in front of the fire for breakfast (unless the day is warm when guests usually eat outside). A narrow, handsome antique staircase leads upstairs to the bedrooms, each lovingly decorated by Martine, who sewed everything herself. The fabrics and wall-covering are all color-coordinated. My favorite is the Green Room with a darling floral-print wallpaper, airy white curtains, and a view out over the back garden. However, it is not the decor or the ambiance that makes a stay here such a delight: Martine and George Langlais truly love having visitors, pampering them as if they were long-time family friends. *Directions:* Onzain is on N152 between Blois and Tours. From Onzain, take D58 west. Just after leaving town, watch for a Citroën shop on your right and, on your left, the Chambres d'Hôtes sign.

CHEZ LANGLAIS (Gîtes de France)
Hosts: Martine & George Langlais
46, Rue de Meuves
41150 Onzain, France
Tel: 02.54.20.78.82 or 06.07.69.74.78, Fax: 02.54.20.78.82
5 rooms, Double: 350F–360F
Open Easter to Nov, Very good English spoken
Region: Loire Valley, Michelin Map 238
www.karenbrown.com/france/chezlanglais.html

Plaisance, although located in a nondescript village, is an enchanting inn and conveniently located just 30 minutes from the Paris, CDG airport—a heavenly spot to begin or end your holiday in France. Relax in total luxury and be pampered by charming Françoise Montrozier—for a fraction of the cost of a hotel in Paris. Plaisance is an adorable, ivy-covered, 13th-century stone cottage, accented by white shutters and a walled garden with lush lawn and beautifully manicured beds of flowers. In the main house there is one large bedroom elegantly decorated in a color scheme of peach and a second smaller bedroom with wood paneling. But splurge and request the deluxe room across the courtyard. This gorgeous room sets all standards for luxury and refinement. The room, with satellite TV, is decorated in pretty tones of pink and rose—a color scheme repeated from the beautiful fabric on the headboards to the sofa, lampshades, drapes, and carpet. The bathroom (like the one in the main house) is incredibly splendid, with fixtures of superb quality. Breakfast, a masterpiece of perfection, displays once again Françoise's (formerly of Maxim's in Paris) passion for excellence. This lodging is truly superb. *Directions:* Located about 20 km northeast of Paris CDG. From the airport take D401 to Dammartin-en-Goele, then D64 to Othis where you follow signs to Beaumarchais. In Beaumarchais, go straight and watch for the Chambres d'Hôtes sign on the right. Ask for a map when making reservations.

PLAISANCE (Gîtes de France)
Hostess: Madame Françoise Montrozier
12, Rue des Suisses
Beaumarchais, 77280 Othis, France
Tel: 01.60.03.33.98, Fax: 01.60.03.56.71
3 rooms, Double: 690F–790F, 1 apt: 890F
Table d'hôte: 245F includes wine, served in guests' room
Closed Feb 15 to 28, Very little English spoken, No smoking
Region: Île de France, Michelin Map 237
www.karenbrown.com/france/plaisance.html

Set center stage in an attractive complex of weathered stone and ivy-covered buildings is the Château de Beaufer. It is a lovely château on an intimate scale dressed with white shutters and complete with end turrets and a gorgeous setting of lawn and surrounding forest. Doorways are framed by climbing roses and geraniums hang heavy from wrought iron balconies. Six attractive, large guestrooms are found in the various buildings. I particularly liked one that shared a climbing stair—dressed in colors of red and cream, it was beautiful, decorated with antiques set on handsome tile floors. I was given a personal tour by the daughter, visiting from their homeland of Switzerland, who claimed her favorite to be a dramatic two-story room whose first level provides a comfortable sofa arrangement and whose loft accommodates a lovely old bed topped with down comforter. Attractive details such as stencil paintings, old furnishings, decorative plates and lovely art are tastefully appointed throughout. Adjacent to the pool, the sitting room, with its exposed loft beams and massive rock fireplace, offers guests a spot to gather and watch television. The pool is gorgeous, set in the old stone walls with vistas out to the surrounding countryside. Breakfast is served on the terrace patio or indoors in the library or in the cozy turret room. The Roggens pride themselves on their bountiful country breakfasts. Friendly dogs shadow the owners and kittens were born the morning we visited. *Directions:* Take the Tournus exit off A6, then travel east on the D14 to Ozenay.

CHÂTEAU DE BEAUFER
Hosts: Family Roggen
Route d'Ozenay, Col de Beaufer
71700 Tournus, France
Tel: 03.85.51.18.24, Fax: 03.85.51.25.04
E-mail: beaufer@aol.com
6 rooms, Double: 720F–900F
Table d'hôte: 150F–250F
Open all year, Credit cards: MC, VS
Fluent English spoken
Region: Burgundy, Michelin Map 243

Château de Messey is one of the best bed and breakfasts in our guide. To begin with, the region is gorgeous—especially fascinating for wine buffs as this is the heart of the Chardonnay wine-producing district. Also, the bed and breakfast's setting is of fairy-tale quality—the adorable stone house, banked by flowers and accented with green shutters, nestles on the edge of a tiny mill stream where a weeping willow shades a rowboat beckoning guests for a lazy excursion. Breakfast and dinner are usually served outside in this hopelessly romantic setting. To add icing to the cake, the spacious guestrooms are all beautifully decorated in antiques and have excellent tiled bathrooms. Even if the above did not entice you to visit, the extraordinary hospitality of the Fachon family would alone suffice as reason to come. As an added bonus, Marie-Laurence is a superb cook. Although called "château," the bed and breakfast is located in a pretty building below the château where the workers used to live (some rooms in the château are available for rent). Bernard works for the charming Dumont family who owns the château (and the bed and breakfast) and can arrange a visit to their winery, which produces a superb Chardonnay. *Directions:* Take A6 south from Beaune to the Tournus exit, then go west on D14 to Ozenay. Go through Ozenay and continue 2 km to Messey where the bed and breakfast is on your left.

CHÂTEAU DE MESSEY
Hosts: Marie-Laurence & Bernard Fachon
Messey, 71700 Ozenay, France
Tel: 03.85.51.33.83 or 03.85.51.16.11, Fax: 03.85.32.57.30
E-mail: bf@golfenfrance.com
5 rooms, Double: 450F–550F
Table d'hôte: 150F per person
Closed Jan & Feb, Credit cards: MC, VS
Good English spoken
Region: Burgundy, Michelin Map 243
www.karenbrown.com/france/chateaudemessey.html

The lovely Chauveau home enjoys an idyllic setting on a hillside overlooking the family vineyards and the distant River Vienne. The fine art of relaxing is easy to master in these luxurious and scenic surroundings where each day begins with fresh croissants and coffee or tea on the terrace overlooking the lush valley. Impeccable taste prevails in the furnishings and decor, creating an elegant country-home ambiance. Madame Chauveau offers one suite with two bedrooms in her home and two more bedrooms in Tourelle, located poolside. Each guestroom enjoys its own private entrance and I was especially charmed by Tourelle Haute with its lovely views of the surrounding vineyards. The decor throughout is very handsome, with stone walls, slate-tile floors, and pretty country antique furniture. Pretty print curtains and matching upholstery complete the pleasing ensemble. The Chauveaus' pool and sunbathing terrace are inviting—perfect for a dip in the early-morning or late afternoon after a day of wine tasting. A stay at Domaine de Beauséjour is truly an experience to be savored. Those on a longer stay might want to consider the spacious two bedroom, one bath self-catering unit. *Directions:* Chinon is located about 46 km southwest of Tours and Panzoult is approximately 12 km east of Chinon. From Chinon, take D21 to Cravant les Côteaux and continue towards Panzoult. The Domaine de Beauséjour is on the left after 2 km—the pretty, light-stone house is on the edge of the woods.

DOMAINE DE BEAUSÉJOUR (Gîtes de France)
Hosts: Marie-Claude & Gérard Chauveau
Panzoult
37220 L'Île Bouchard, France
Tel: 02.47.58.64.64, Fax: 02.47.95.27.13
3 rooms, Double: 450F–500F, Suite: 600F–680F
No table d'hôte
Open all year, Good English spoken
Region: Loire Valley, Michelin Map 232
www.karenbrown.com/france/domainedebeausejour.html

Your charming hosts, Robert Chappell and Stuart Shippey (who are English), were on holiday when they discovered Le Moulin Neuf and they bought it on the spot. Of course, it didn't look anything like it does today—they have poured their love and immense talent into creating a dream. Robert and Stuart live in an enchanting stone house on the property. Next door, a cozy cottage (dedicated to guests) has an ever-so-appealing lounge with yellow walls and yellow-and-green-floral drapes accenting comfortable sofas grouped around an enormous walk-in fireplace. There are six prettily decorated bedrooms, each with a tranquil view of the parklike grounds. Meticulously tended flowerbeds abound and the old mill stream loops lazily through lush grass dappled with shade from large trees. Completing this idyllic scene is a romantic pond. Dotting the lawn are lounge chairs where guests relax in utter peace, only occasionally disturbed by a duck waddling by, a visit from Fergie the rooster, or perhaps a nuzzle from Benji or Foston, the adorable dogs. Le Moulin Neuf is truly a very special bed and breakfast and the price is remarkably low for such fine quality and outstanding charm. *Directions:* From Limeuil, take the D31 for the Cingle de Limeuil. After passing the Cingle de Limeuil, continue down the hill then at the crossroads go straight on D2 towards Saint-Alvère. Fork left after 100 meters and continue about 2 km. The sign for Le Moulin Neuf is on the left-hand side.

LE MOULIN NEUF
Hosts: Robert Chappell & Stuart Shippey
Paunat, 24510 Sainte Alvère, France
Tel: 05.53.63.30.18, Fax: 05.53.73.33.91
E-mail: moulin-neuf@usa.net
6 rooms, Double: 394F
No table d'hôte
Open all year (winter by reservation), Fluent English spoken
Region: Dordogne, Michelin Map 233
www.karenbrown.com/france/lemoulinneuf.html

Jane and Geoff Bramfitt owned a home in England in Stratford-upon-Avon with dreams of turning it into a small hotel. But one year, while on holiday in Brittany, they fell in love with a turn-of-the-century house overlooking the coast with an idyllic sandy cove just down the road. They bought it, moved to France, and in 1991 opened a bed and breakfast with three rooms (each with a sea view). Jane and Geoff are super hosts, pampering their guests and making them feel like friends of the family. They work as a team: Jane maintains high standards of housekeeping with beautifully laundered, crisp linens, quality towels, and spotlessly clean rooms while Geoff (whose mother was a chef) has a passion for cooking and prepares such delicious meals that guests return eagerly in anticipation of what's for dinner. Seafood is one of Geoff's specialties and you will frequently find him out fishing for the evening meal—often with a guest in tow! Ty Pesketer is not fancy: just simple rooms, old-fashioned comfort, unpretentious friendliness, and great prices. The prize is the bedroom on the top floor—it has two cozy rooms of almost equal size (one is the bedroom, the other the bathroom), both with little balconies with a view. The other two bedrooms (which are less expensive) share a bathroom. *Directions:* From N12 take D42 to Plestin les Grèves. Go through town to the stoplight then continue straight ahead, turning right at the harbor. Go about 2 km, watching for a sign on the left to Ty Pesketer.

TY PESKETER
Hosts: Jane & Geoff Bramfitt
Pors Mellec
22310 Plestin Les Grèves, France
Tel: 02.96.35.09.98, Fax: none
3 rooms, Double: 280F–350F
Table d'hôte: 90F per person
Open Apr to Nov, Fluent English spoken
Region: Brittany, Michelin Map 230
www.karenbrown.com/france/typesketer.html

The Manoir de Kergrec'h, located on the northern coast of Brittany, is a superb 17th-century manor, impressively large, yet tremendously inviting—especially in early summer when a profusion of old-fashioned pink roses lace and soften the stern gray-stone exterior. The most outstanding attribute of the Manoir de Kergrec'h is its splendid setting in an enormous park that stretches to the sea, an absolute paradise for walking. When you enter into the large front hallway, to the right is a very formal, beautiful living room. To the left is a handsome dining room with beautiful parquet floors in a herringbone pattern and a massive fireplace which soars almost to the ceiling. A spiral stone staircase, worn with the footsteps of time, winds up through the tower to the bedrooms which are most attractively decorated with color-coordinated fabrics and gorgeous antique furniture. All the bedrooms are appealing, but my particular favorite is located on the top floor. It is a real gem and especially cozy, with gabled windows and a delicate floral-print wallpaper in tones of rose and green. All of the bedrooms have large, modern bathrooms. *Directions:* Located on the northern coast of Brittany. Exit the N12 at Guingamp and go north to Treguier. From Treguier take D8 north for 7 km to Plougrescant. Turn right just beyond the quaint old church, continue a short distance, and you will see the stately manor on your right.

MANOIR DE KERGREC'H
Hosts: Vicomte & Vicomtesse de Roquefeuil
22820 Plougrescant, France
Tel: 02.96.92.59.13, Fax: 02.96.92.51.27
6 rooms, Double: 500F–600F, Suite: 750F–900F
Table d'hôte: from 200F per person (served occasionally)
Open all year
Some English spoken
Region: Brittany, Michelin Map 230
www.karenbrown.com/france/manoirdekergrech.html

Les Tuillières is a rare find. This gem of a 16th-century stone farmhouse has everything—superb hosts with boundless warmth of welcome, lovely flower gardens, spacious bedrooms with super-comfortable mattresses, appealing decor, a gorgeous setting, large heated swimming pool, and delicious meals served with produce straight from the garden. Being located a bit "off the beaten path" makes a stay here even more special—without Les Tuillières as a target, you would probably never accidentally roam into this breathtakingly beautiful niche of northern Provence. Although within easy reach of such well-known cities as Avignon, Montélimar, and Orange, this is a sunny, quiet area of lavender, sunflowers, vineyards, and sleepy villages. From the moment you walk into Les Tuillières' courtyard, your heart will be won. Ivy laces the honey-toned stone home with its white trim and green shutters, roses and geraniums add a dash of color, while lavender scents the air. Hermann Jenny (who is Swiss) was formerly a top executive in hotel management, so knowing how to please guests is second nature to him. Susan (who is American) has a natural gift of hospitality and pampers her guests like cherished friends. Hermann is your superb chef and on most days dinner is served under the stars in the romantic garden. *Directions*: From the south take the A7 to Montélimar Sud exit. Follow signs to Dieulefit, go through the village of La Batie Rolland and into La Bégude de Mazeuc where you turn left on D9 until Charols. Turn right in Charols on D128 for about 2 km. Les Tuillières is on the right.

LES TUILLIÈRES
Hosts: Susan & Hermann Jenny
26160 Pont de Barret, France
Tel & fax: 04.75.90.43.91
E-mail: h.jen@infonie.fr
6 rooms, Double: 425F–460F
Table d'hôte: 150F per person, includes wine
Open Easter to Nov
Fluent English spoken
Region: Provence-Drôme, Michelin Map 245

La Métairie Basse, a simple yet superb bed and breakfast, is just on the on the outskirts of Hameau de Prouilhe, a tranquil village nestled in the densely wooded hills of the beautiful Parc Naturel Régional du Haut Languedoc. Here your welcome will be as genuine as this working farm, where sheep are raised and chestnuts and walnuts harvested. One of the characterful stone farm buildings has been meticulously restored and is now totally for guests' use. It has a private terrace in front where Eliane serves an excellent breakfast. From the terrace, you enter into a small, spotlessly clean parlor with a well-equipped kitchen on one side where guests are welcome to fix themselves a light meal. Down the hall are two meticulously kept, very attractive guestrooms. Each is similar, exuding a country flair, with thick stone walls, planked wooden-pegged floors, antique armoires, and handmade crocheted curtains. Both guestrooms are decorated in excellent taste using pretty fabrics and antique furniture. At La Métairie Basse you're truly off the beaten path, but the quality of accommodation is so exceptional that you will be amazed at the price. *Directions:* From Carcassonne take the D118 north to Mazamet and then the N112 east to Courniou. From Courniou, turn north on the D169 for 3 km towards Prouilhe. The Chambres d'Hôtes sign is well displayed, marking the entrance to the bed and breakfast on the left before you reach the town.

LA MÉTAIRIE BASSE (Gîtes de France)
Hosts: Eliane & Jean-Louis Lunes
Hameau de Prouilhe
34220 Courniou, France
Tel & fax: 04.67.97.21.59
2 rooms, Double: 270F
No table d'hôte
Open Apr to Oct, Some English spoken
Region: Haut Languedoc, Michelin Map 235
www.karenbrown.com/france/lametairiebasse.html

Pont du Gard, the ancient, three-tiered stone aqueduct spanning the Le Gardon river, is one of France's star attractions and La Terre des Lauriers offers bed and breakfast within walking distance of this impressive sight. The house, beautifully situated in 13 acres of parkland, is typical of the region, with a tan stucco exterior, tiled roof, and brown shutters. This is not a spiffy, decorator-perfect place, but rather exudes a homelike, lived-in ambiance that reflects the warmth and personality of your charming host, Gérard Cristini, who welcomes everyone as friends. Gérard is a passionate fisherman, as photos and knickknacks about the house attest. Each of the bedrooms has its own personality and the benefit of a small balcony looking over the large swimming pool and out to the forest. On the same floor as the bedrooms there is an intimate parlor, which is solely for the use of the guests. One of the delights of staying at La Terre des Lauriers is its location: from the garden you can wander down a path through a dense forest of poplar, laurel, bamboo, and oak trees to the river. *Directions*: From the A9 (north of Nîmes) take exit 23 following signs to Remoulins and Pont du Gard. Go through Remoulins, cross the river, and turn right to Pont du Gard–Rive Droite. Before you reach Pont du Gard, watch for a sign to La Terre des Lauriers on your right.

LA TERRE DES LAURIERS
Host: Gérard Cristini
Rive Droite–Pont du Gard
30210 Remoulins, France
Tel & fax: 04.66.37.19.45
4 rooms, Double: 420F
No table d'hôte
Open Mar to Oct
Very good English spoken
Region: Provence, Michelin Map 245

Bed & Breakfast Descriptions   105

Riquewihr is a beguiling walled town with cobbled streets, timbered facades, and steeply pitched slate-and-tile roofs—all set against a backdrop of green vineyards, an ideal base from which to explore the Alsatian wine route. We could not find an appropriate chambre d'hôte but we were pleased to discover on a charming cobbled street within the town walls, the family-run Hotel Saint Nicholas. We were escorted on a tour of the rooms by the daughter and, overseeing the dining room, the father was ever-present to attend to our needs. The restaurant is quite handsome with high-back chairs upholstered in a regal green-and-rust stripe. Local specialties are featured on the menu as well as wines from local vintners—the village of Riquewihr alone boasts 100 wine makers. Guestrooms are found in the building across from the restaurant which is where, typically, inquiries about rooms and reservations need to be addressed. In the hotel wing we climbed an attractive staircase whose wall was painted with murals of regional scenes and found the guestrooms to be comfortable, but quite basic in their amenities and decor. The Hotel Saint Nicholas offers the traveler a great value but very simple accommodation. You can stay at the hotel *en pension* or simply opt for room and breakfast. *Directions*: Riquewihr is located on the D3 just west off the D10, south of Ribeauvillé. The town is closed to vehicles, so it is necessary to park on the outside of the town wall. The Hotel Saint Nicholas is accessed most easily from the tower gate.

HOTEL SAINT NICHOLAS
Host: André Schneider
2, Rue St. Nicholas
68340 Riquewihr, France
Tel:03.89.49.01.51, Fax: 03.89.49.04.36
33 rooms, Double: 356F, Demi pension: 270F per person
Restaurant
Open Apr to Jan, Credit cards: MC, VS
Some English spoken
Region: Alsace, Michelin Map 242

The beautiful 18th-century Château de Montgouverne is located just outside of Tours, yet it seems you are far from the city and deep in the countryside once you enter into the parklike grounds. The two-story, ivy-covered manor with steeply pitched slate roof looks straight out of a fairy tale—it is just as inviting and pretty as can be. Happily, the interior is no disappointment. The rooms continue the romantic mood, being totally furnished in handsome antiques and enhanced by opulent, swagged drapes of fine fabric framing the views from each window. Thanks to the clever long, narrow design of the house, all of the lounges and dining room have windows on two sides which capture idyllic views of the gardens. The bedrooms, too, are splendidly decorated. Several are in the main house, the rest in an adjacent building that was once used for the processing of the grapes. From the exterior, this "annex" looks much more rustic than the château, but this only makes it wonderfully surprising to find these rooms are just as elegant as those in the main house. As an added bonus after a day of sightseeing, there is a swimming pool for guests' use tucked in the garden. JUST AS WE WERE GOING TO PRESS WE WERE NOTIFIED THAT THE CHÂTEAU HAD BEEN SOLD AND THAT THE PROPERTY WILL NO LONGER BE OFFERING BED & BREAKFAST.

CHÂTEAU DE MONTGOUVERNE (Gîtes de France)
Hosts: Christine & Jacques Desvignes
37210 Rochecorbon, France
Tel: 02.47.52.84.59, Fax: 02.47.52.84.61
6 rooms, Double: 590F–790F, Suite: 790F–1,050F
No table d'hôte
Open all year
Credit cards: all major
Good English spoken
Region: Loire Valley, Michelin Map 238

The medieval town of Rochefort en Terre, with its fortified château, narrow cobbled streets, and antique shops, is enchanting. Nestled on 20 acres of park just minutes from the heart of town is the gorgeous and luxurious Château de Talhouet, truly an attraction in its own right. A beautiful forested drive leads to a handsome entry with an absolutely spectacular salon beyond. This striking, wood-paneled room was the place where the judge once held court—the spot where he sat and passed judgement is now enclosed by glass and the fireplace is now a deep, arched doorway into a beautiful dining room where tables are set intimately for two. Beyond the billiard room is a beautiful, spacious guest living room with gorgeous fabrics draping the full-length windows and lovely hand-painted beams. Most guestrooms are found up a stone stairway with a dramatic 16th-century wood gate. Chambre d'Honneur is a twin-bedded room with a large armoire and a view of the stunning grounds. LouisXV is a smaller room with a draped canopy over a queen bed and a table set at the window. Louis XIII has twin beds and a table with high-backed chairs at the fireplace. The Montgolfière has gold stripes with dark furnishings. The Directoire, a twin under lowered ceilings, is not in keeping with the ambiance of the château, and Bleue is plainer. Up a back staircase are a few more simple rooms. *Directions*: Leave Rochefort en Terre in the direction of Pleucadeuc on the D774. The Talhouet is signposted 2 km from town and located at the end of a long road.

CHÂTEAU DE TALHOUET   **New**
Host: Jean Pol Soulein
56220 Rochefort en Terre, France
Tel: 02.97.43.34.72, Fax: 02.97.43.35.04
8 rooms, Double: 700F–1000F
Table d'hôte: 230F per person
Open all year, Credit cards: MC, VS
Very little English spoken
Region: Brittany, Michelin Map: 230

The comfort offered by the elegant Château de la Commanderie challenges that of the finest hotels. Comte and Comtesse de Jouffroy-Gonsans obviously take great pride and pleasure in welcoming guests to their historic home, which has been in the Comte's family since 1630. His gracious wife has redecorated the entire castle with impeccable taste, utilizing beautifully complementing color schemes in upholstery fabrics and wallpapers. Lovely collectibles, antiques, and objets d'art grace the bedrooms and public areas. Warm, personal touches such as bowls of potpourri, cologne, bath gels, and soaps add comfort and convenience to the modern bathrooms. In the evening, the Comte and Comtesse serve an aperitif in the salon before the fire, and then escort guests into an elegant dining room and host a delightful dinner party. A stay with the de Jouffroy-Gonsans is a chance to experience a taste of aristocratic country life. Hunting and riding parties are also available, season permitting, and a beautiful flower garden is open to visitors. There are beautiful castles and gardens to visit in the area as well as two golf courses. *Directions:* Farges-Allichamps is about 35 km south of Bourges. From Bourges, travel south towards Montluçon on N144. Turn off before the town of Saint Amand-Montrond at Bruère-Allichamps and follow signs to Farges-Allichamps. Château de la Commanderie is signposted. If approaching from the A71, take the Saint Amand exit—the château is 7 km from the freeway.

CHÂTEAU DE LA COMMANDERIE
Hosts: Comte & Comtesse de Jouffroy-Gonsans
Farges-Allichamps
18200 Saint Amand-Montrond, France
Tel: 02.48.61.04.19, Fax: 02.48.61.01.84
E-mail: commanderie@ila-chateau.com
9 rooms & suites, Double: 800F–1,200F, Suite: 1,200F
Table d'hôte: 350F per person, includes wine
Open all year (winter by reservation), Credit cards: AX, VS
Little English spoken
Region: Berry, Michelin Map 238
www.karenbrown.com/france/chateaudelacommanderie.html

Saint Clar's market place is enclosed by charming arcaded buildings. In the center of the square stands a wonderful 14th-century covered market, officially designated as a historic monument. Also on the plaza is the old town hall: hence its name, *Place de la Mairie*. Nicole and Jean-Francois Cournot are a gracious, artistic couple who live in one of the buildings facing the square. When they renovated the house, they converted part of their home as a bed and breakfast. You enter through an arched stone doorway into a wide hall, formerly horse stables, and ascend a stone stairway to the next floor. Nicole has tastefully decorated the guestrooms (which are in a separate wing of the house) in a charming, attractive style, using pretty Laura Ashley fabrics and wallpapers throughout. Guests are welcome to relax in a lovely salon with a marble fireplace flanked by comfortable chairs and couch. There is also a large garden in back where guests can relax. Breakfast is served in the cozy kitchen with a blue-and-white-tiled floor and country antique furnishings. *Directions:* Saint Clar is located about 40 km south of Agen. From the A62, take exit 8, marked Valence d'Agen. Go south on D953 following signs to Saint Clar. In Saint Clar, look for Place de la Mairie, the square with the medieval market in the center. It's a small town, so it will be easy to find. The hotel faces the square.

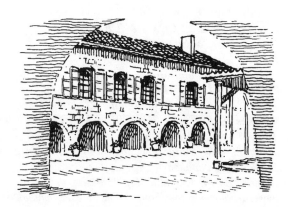

CHEZ COURNOT (Gîtes de France)
Hosts: Nicole & Jean-Francois Cournot
Place de la Mairie
32380 Saint Clar, France
Tel: 05.62.66.47.31, Fax: 05.62.66.47.70
E-mail: nicole.cournot@wanadoo.fr
2 rooms, Double: 280F, 1 suite: 320F
Table d'hôte: 90F per person, includes wine
Open all year, Some English spoken
Region: Tarn, Michelin Map 235

Martine and Jacques Lefebvre's romantic, ivy-clad home with creamy-white shutters and an enclosed front garden is reminiscent of a pretty English house. The inside is as attractive as the exterior. Martine, your charming hostess, used to own an antique shop and her cozy, picture-perfect parlor abounds with antiques, including a round table, grandfather clock, superb armoire, and two handsome needlepoint chairs. Martine's excellent taste is also reflected in the guestrooms. My favorite, the Blue Room, has windows on both sides, capturing the first morning sun and the last evening light. The floor is terra cotta, the ceiling beamed, the furnishings antique, and the bed and windows draped in a blue-and-white fabric. The jovial Jacques Lefebvre teaches horse-and-carriage driving. If booked ahead, for a reasonable price he takes guests on an all-day sightseeing excursion by carriage, accompanied by a picnic packed by Martine. What a magical way for four or more people to explore the splendid countryside—I can hardly wait to try it. *Directions:* From Paris take the A11 southwest. Just beyond Le Mans Nord, take the A81 (towards Rennes). At the first exit (Joué en Charnie), go south on D4 to Sable/Sarthe, then take D309 (towards Angers) for 9 km to Saint Denis d'Anjou. As you near town, take the first road to the left, signposted Chambres d'Hôtes. The house is on the right.

LE LOGIS ET LES ATTELAGES DU RAY (Gîtes de France)
Hosts: Martine & Jacques Lefebvre
53290 Saint Denis d'Anjou, France
Tel: 02.43.70.64.10, Fax: 02.43.70.65.53
3 rooms, Double: 350F–395F
Table d'hôte (some Saturdays): 160F per person, includes wine
Open all year, Credit cards: MC, VS
Very good English spoken by Madame
Region: Pays de la Loire, Michelin Map 232
www.karenbrown.com/france/lelogisduray.html

Having spent most of her life in the country, Madeleine Rousseau found living in an apartment in the city much too confining, so she bought Le Four à Pain, a 200-year-old farmhouse just on the outskirts of Saint Denis Le Ferment. The timbered home with steeply pitched roof was almost a ruin, but Madeleine has transformed it into an ever-so-pretty bed and breakfast. Large wooden gates open from the street onto a graveled courtyard and a meticulously tended garden. The back of the property gently slopes down the hillside where apple trees dot the green lawn. The spotlessly tidy lounge has a dining table for breakfast set at one end and a sitting area around the fireplace at the other. Wooden steps lead up to one of the two guestrooms, which is spacious and has a large bathroom. However, the choice accommodation is in the doll-house-like cottage in the garden where the bread used to be baked for the farm—one wall still has the original oven, the other walls are covered in a very pretty wallpaper of tiny red roses and spring flowers. The cottage also has a kitchenette and a quiet sitting area under the trees. *Note:* The picture below depicts only the cottage and not the main house. *Directions*: From Paris take A15 north for about 35 km, then D915 (near Pontoise) north to Gisors, then D14 to Bezu Saint Eloi (5 km), where you turn right on the D17 to Saint Denis. After 1.4 km on the D17, in the village center, turn left at the Bed and Breakfast sign (at this place the road is close to the river). Go up the hill and Le Four à Pain is on your right.

LE FOUR À PAIN
Hostess: Madeleine Rousseau
8, Rue de Gruchets
27140 Saint Denis Le Ferment, France
Tel: 02.32.55.14.45, Fax: none
2 rooms, Double: 250F–310F
No table d'hôte
Open all year, Some English spoken
Region: Normandy, Michelin Map 231
www.karenbrown.com/france/lefourapain.html

Your exceptionally gracious hosts, Denyse and Bernard Betts, left their native Canada to move to the beautiful Haute-Savoie region of France. Upon arrival, they began looking for a spacious house with lots of character, in a beautiful setting, suitable for a deluxe bed and breakfast. Forty-nine houses later they found "it"—a 200-year-old Savoyard farmhouse perched on a hill between the Alps and the Jura mountains. Although Les Bruyères' heritage is a farm, there is nothing rustic about these accommodations. Each suite has a large bedroom opening onto a sitting room, antique furniture, fine mattresses, beautiful linens, spacious modern bathrooms, and elegant fabrics. One room is fresh and pretty with color-coordinating fabrics which are predominantly blue and white with accents of yellow. The second suite is ever-so-romantic, with dark raspberry-colored wallpaper setting off to perfection an antique writing desk, green slip-covered chairs, and a lovely floral bedspread. As an added bonus, Denyse is an outstanding chef whose meals are both delicious and beautiful. *Directions:* Located between Annecy and Aix-Les-Bains. From the A41 take exit 15 towards Rumilly and almost immediately turn left onto RN201, signposted Saint Félix. In front of the church in Saint Félix, take the only road and just after the cemetery, turn left up the hill towards Mercy. At the statue, turn right, then immediately left, then left again into Les Bruyères.

LES BRUYÈRES (Gîtes de France)
Hosts: Denyse & Bernard Betts
Mercy, 74540 Saint FélixFrance
Tel: 04.50.60.96.53, Fax: 04.50.60.94.65
3 suites, Double: 650F, 2-night minimum
Maisonette available for weekly rental
Table d'hôte: 200F per person, includes wine
Open all year, Credit cards: MC, VS
Fluent English spoken, No smoking
Region: Haute-Savoie, Michelin Map 244
www.karenbrown.com/france/lesbruyeres.html

Set in the mystical marshlands of coastal Normandy, La Ferme de la Rivière is an imposing fortified farmhouse dating from the 16th century. The main entry leads directly into an old tower and up a well-worn spiral staircase to the dining room. The friendly Marie family serves dinners as well as breakfasts in this warm, inviting room with its atmospheric stone floors, walk-in fireplace, and country furniture. Bedrooms are found upstairs—most have enchanting views over the surrounding fields and marshes. Two of the bedrooms are quite large, share a bath and WC, and can be rented as a suite. The two smaller bedrooms have an intimate charm all their own, and each has a private shower and WC. All of the bedrooms are simply furnished, mostly in family antiques. La Ferme de la Rivière is a rare find, offering charming, comfortable accommodations, delicious country cuisine, peaceful scenery, and a warm family welcome. *Directions:* Saint Germain du Pert is located 28 km west of Bayeux via N13. Exit N13 onto D113 at La Cambe and take D113 south about 1 km to D124. Turn right onto D124. Go about 1 km to the Maries' gate, signposted on the left.

LA FERME DE LA RIVIÈRE (Gîtes de France)
Hosts: Paulette & Hervé Marie
14230 Saint Germain du Pert, France
Tel: 02.31.22.72.92, Fax: 02.31.22.01.63
3 rooms, Double: from 260F
Table d'hôte: 90F per person, includes cider
Open Apr to Nov
Very little English spoken
Region: Normandy, Michelin Map 231
www.karenbrown.com/france/lafermedelariviere.html

Chalet Rémy is an adorable 18th-century stone-and-wood farmhouse perched way up in the mountains with a view over the valley to the extraordinary summit of Mont Blanc. A profusion of flowers surrounds the house and geraniums grace the balconies. Chalet Rémy is particularly famous as a restaurant and on sunny days, the terrace is brimming with families who have come to enjoy a wonderful meal there, surrounded by nature at its finest. The guestrooms all open onto a gallery which looks down upon the floor below. Be forewarned: the accommodations are small and quite basic—staying here is a bit like camping out in a mountain lodge. Each room has a sink, but all share showers and toilets "down the hall." If luxury is important to you, this would not be an appropriate choice, but for location and old-fashioned natural charm, this wonderful "restaurant with rooms" just can't be beaten. Chalet Rémy is owned by Madame Didier who is assisted in the management by her charming daughter, Frédérique, while her talented niece holds sway in the kitchen. *Directions:* Take D909 from Mègeve towards Saint Gervais. Just before coming to Saint Gervais, turn right on D43 signposted to Saint Nicholas and Le Bettex. Continue winding up the road, following signs for Le Bettex where you will see signs for Chalet Rémy.

CHALET RÉMY
Hostess: Mme Micheline Didier
Le Bettex, 74170 Saint Gervais, France
Tel: 04.50.93.11.85, Fax: 04.50.93.14.45
19 rooms, Double: 320F
Open all year
Credit cards: MC, VS
No table d'hôte, restaurant open daily
Good English spoken by Frédérique
Region: Haute-Savoie, Michelin Map 244
www.karenbrown.com/france/chaletremy.html

"Indeo" is a secluded jewel, truly a rare find for the traveler seeking decorator-perfect decor, stunning architectural design, award-winning gardens, a swimming pool hidden in a romantic walled garden, memorable dining, and genuine warmth of welcome. Nicole Henderson is an exceptionally talented interior designer and her English husband is an architect whose career has led them to exotic places around the world. Before retirement, their home for ten years was Korea. During that period Nicole collected superb Oriental artifacts which she has blended skillfully with colorful Provençal fabrics and antiques from her native France. The result is so stunning that "Indeo" has been featured in full-color spreads in many prominent home and architectural magazines. The bed and breakfast is located in a cluster of centuries-old stone farmhouses, romantically nestled in a wooded hamlet. Guests have their own charming stone cottage with artistically decorated bedrooms which are not large, but do not need to be since they share a spacious living room which is as comfortable as it is beautiful, along with a flower-laden terrace. *Directions:* From Ales take D981 southeast towards Uzès. After about 15 km, turn left on D7, then right on D339 towards Vacquieres. Turn right again at the first asphalt road and continue down the hill. After you pass under a stone archway, "Indeo" is the first house on your right, with yellow shutters and a discreet sign.

"INDEO"
Hostess: Nicole Henderson
Hameau de Vacquières
30580 Saint Just et Vacquières, France
Tel: 04.66.83.70.75, Fax: 04.66.83.74.15
5 rooms, Double: 580F
Table d'hôte: 200F per person, includes wine
Open all year, Credit cards: VS
Fluent English spoken, No children, No smoking
Region: Languedoc, Michelin Map 245
www.karenbrown.com/france/indeo.html

The pretty, old complex of La Croix de la Voulte is built of white regional stone and dates from the 15th and 17th centuries. All the guest bedrooms are found in an independent wing and are newly renovated with much attention to detail. A high level of comfort prevails; each room has a private bathroom, soft Pakistani carpets covering the stone floors, and luxurious bedding to assure a good night's sleep. Each room has a private entry and special character all its own. Anjou, the largest bedroom, is very regal, with a massive old stone fireplace, four-poster bed, old armoire, and tapestry chairs. And I adored Périgord, painted in a warm yellow and enjoying the advantage of an end/corner location. Low, beamed ceilings, light-stone walls, and lovely antique furniture add historical character to all the bedrooms. There is a tranquil courtyard, a park with a pond, and a sunny terrace in front of the swimming pool, a pleasant place to enjoy a leisurely breakfast. Guests may also elect to pamper themselves by bringing ice buckets and glasses that they find in their rooms to the poolside to enjoy a drink. *Directions:* Saint Lambert des Levées is located about 5 km west of Saumur on the north bank of the Loire. Take D229 in the direction of Saint Lambert des Levées and Château de Boumois. Pass the Saumur train station and continue 4 km until you see the sign "La Croix de la Voulte" directing you to turn into a driveway on the right. This is a gem.

LA CROIX DE LA VOULTE (*Gîtes de France*)
Hosts: Helga & Jean Pierre Minder
Saint Lambert des Levées
49400 Saumur, France
Tel & fax: 02.41.38.46.66
4 rooms, Double: 420F–520F
No table d'hôte
Open Easter to Oct, Fluent English & German spoken
Region: Loire Valley, Michelin Map 232
www.karenbrown.com/france/lacroixdelavoulte.html

Le Moulin de Linthe, hugging the banks of the River Sarthe, has an idyllic setting. While the mill dates back several hundred years, most of what you see today is an ingenious reconstruction by Claude Rollini. For three months he hauled stones from the riverbed, which he used (along with old beams, bricks, and antique paneling) to rebuild the mill. The result is a charming cottage-style bed and breakfast with gabled windows accented by a red-tiled roof. Within there is a cozy parlor with a large window looking out to the slowly turning waterwheel. Most of the bedrooms overlook the old mill pond and an enchanting view of the meandering river. Ask for the corner bedroom decorated in soft pinks and greens for it has captivating views in two directions. Jackie prepares a breakfast with homemade jams, and Claude (who was a chef in Chicago for two years) prepares dinner. Don't be surprised while dining if several ducks waddle by the dining-room window. In addition to sweet accommodations and ever-so-friendly hosts, there is another bonus—fishing along a 2.5 km stretch of the Sarthe river where trout and pike abound. *Directions:* Head southwest from Paris on A10/A11 to Le Mans, then turn north on N138 in the direction of Alençon. When you come to Beaumont-sur-Sarthe, take the D39 to Fresnay-sur-Sarthe, and the D15 to Saint Leonard des Bois. As you enter the village, take the first road on your left to Le Moulin de Linthe.

LE MOULIN DE LINTHE (Gîtes de France)
Hosts: Jackie & Claude Rollini
72130 Saint Leonard des Bois, France
Tel & fax: 02.43.33.79.22
5 rooms, Double: 350F
Table d'hôte: 100F per person, includes wine
Open all year, Good English spoken
Region: Normandy, Michelin Map 231
www.karenbrown.com/france/lemoulindelinthe.html

La Pastourelle is a low, stone farmhouse whose style is typical of the Brittany region. A pleasing construction is formed by gray stones of varying sizes mortared together in a seemingly haphazard manner: in fact it is easy to pick out one large boulder that was simply left in place and incorporated into the front wall of the house. The Lédés live in a separate wing of their pretty farmhouse, offering guests an independent entry, salon, dining room, and six guest bedrooms. In charge of the Gîtes for her region, Madame Lédé displays great warmth and charm. An appealing, country ambiance is felt throughout, created by Madame's collection of lovely antiques and special touches such as wildflower bouquets. The bedrooms are spotlessly clean and tastefully decorated with dainty flower-print wallpaper, softly colored carpets, and crocheted bedspreads. Delicious table d'hôte dinners are served downstairs in the cozy dining room and often include local fish or grilled meats and regional specialties such as crêpes. *Directions:* Saint Lormel is located approximately 66 km northwest of Rennes, near the town of Plancoet. From Plancoet, travel north on D768 for 1 km, then turn left onto D19 towards Saint Lormel. On the edge of the village, look for Chambres d'Hôtes signs indicating La Pastourelle which will lead to the Lédés' Breton farmhouse.

LA PASTOURELLE (Gîtes de France)
Hostess: Madame Lédé
Saint Lormel
22130 Plancoet, France
Tel & fax: 02.96.84.03.77
6 rooms, Double: 250F–280F
Table d'hôte: 90F per person, includes wine
Open Mar to Nov 15
Very little English spoken
Region: Brittany, Michelin Map 230
www.karenbrown.com/france/lapastourelle.html

The Château de Vergières' magic begins as you approach by way of a tree-lined lane ending at the stately, three-story manor whose pastel façade is accented by white-shuttered windows and heavy-tiled roof. The rather formal exterior belies the warmth of welcome one finds within. For many years the château has been in the family of Marie-Andrée who has opened her heart and home to guests from all over the world. She is ably assisted by her gracious husband, Jean Pincedé. Inside as well as outside, the château reflects the patina of age and has an ambiance of homey comfort. Quality country antiques are everywhere, yet nothing is contrived, cutely redone, or decorator-perfect. The dining room is especially outstanding with its beamed ceiling, fabulous antique armoires, sideboard, and long wooden table surrounded by Provençal-style wooden chairs. Be sure to plan ahead so you can have the fun of sharing a meal here with your fellow guests. Since our original visit, a swimming pool has been added. *Note:* Château de Vergières has received an award from the World Wildlife Fund for its protection of nature (binoculars, books, and lists of birds, insects, and plants are available for the use of guests). *Directions:* Exit A54 at Saint Martin de Crau (exit 11), take D24 towards Fos sur Mer. After 3 km, watch for a sign on the right side of the road to Vergières. Turn left at the sign. Continue for 3km to the lane leading to the château.

CHÂTEAU DE VERGIÈRES
Hostess: Marie-Andrée Pincedé
Vergières, 13310 Saint Martin de Crau, France
Tel: 04.90.47.17.16, Fax: 04.90.47.38.30
E-mail: vergieres@vergieres.com
6 rooms, Double: 850F–950F
Table d'hôte: 310F per person, includes wine
Open all year, Credit cards: all major
Very good English spoken
Region: Provence, Michelin Maps 240, 245
www.karenbrown.com/france/chateaudevergieres.html

Michel and Josette Garret are former prize-winning dairy farmers who now offer bed and breakfast in their home in a lovely pastoral region north of Bordeaux. Although neither speaks English, their exuberant warmth of welcome overcomes all language barriers. The farmhouse is built in the typical regional style: long and low, of pretty warm-toned stone, accented by white shutters. The interior has been completely renovated, preserving the heavy-beamed ceilings, exposing the light-stone walls, and adding cool tiled floors and modern bathrooms. Sharing an avid interest in local history and regional antiques, the Garrets have filled their home with lovely old pieces such as a huge Bordeaux armoire, a Louis XIV mantelpiece, and a cherry-wood grandfather clock. Bedrooms are nicely furnished and enhanced by French doors leading out to bucolic pasturelands. Ask for the best bedroom—it has recently been beautifully redecorated and has a fabulous new bathroom that surpasses those often found in deluxe hotels. It costs a bit more, but is an astounding value. *Directions*: Leave Bordeaux on the N89 towards Libourne. Then take D910 to Saint Denis de Pile where you turn left at the *mairie* (town hall) onto D22 going over the bridge towards Bonzac. After Bonzac continue on D22 for 1.8 km then turn to the right on a small road marked Gaudart Buisson. Go 700 meters to a Chambres d'Hôtes sign and turn left—the Garrets' house is 200 meters farther on at the end of the driveway.

CHEZ GARRET (Gîtes de France)
Hosts: Josette & Michel Garret
Saint Martin de Laye
33910 Saint Denis de Pile, France
Tel: 05.57.49.41.37, Fax: none
3 rooms, Double: 220F–260F
Table d'hôte: 95F per person, includes wine*
*Dinner not served Jul & Aug
Open end of Apr to Oct, No English spoken
Region: Atlantic Coast, Michelin Map 233
www.karenbrown.com/france/chezgarret.html

Claudine is the busy mother of two children, but runs her bed and breakfast with quiet efficiency and professionalism. The two-story white stone house, located just across the street from the Loire, has belonged to her late husband's family for over 150 years. Behind the house there is a garden where Claudine grows fresh vegetables for her home-cooked dinners. Inside, the house is basic: a central hallway that opens to a dining room on the left which also has a lounge area with sofa and chairs for guests. There are four bedrooms upstairs in the main house, each with its own bathroom. Ask for the corner bedroom in the back. This has a pretty, floral-print wallpaper, an antique bed, a beautiful armoire, and windows on two sides, which make it especially bright and cheerful. Two more double rooms and a suite are found in a separate building facing the back courtyard. For those of you who do not expect everything to be decorator-perfect and like the idea of sharing the family home of an exceptionally gracious, hard-working young hostess, Le Bouquetterie makes a very good choice. *Directions:* From Saumur, take D952 west along the Loire for 25 km. About 1 km after the center of Saint Mathurin-sur-Loire, you see the Piniers' home on your right.

LE BOUQUETTERIE (Gîtes de France) **New**
Hostess: Claudine Pinier
118, Rue du Roi Rene
49250 Saint Mathurin-sur-Loire, France
Tel: 02.41.57.02.00, Fax: 02.41.57.31.90
7 rooms, Double: 300F–350F, Suite: 520F
Table d'hôte: 125F per person, includes wine
Open all year
Good English spoken
Region: Loire Valley, Michelin Map 232

La Ferme des Poiriers Roses is an absolute dream. This quaint Normandy farmhouse features a picture-perfect façade—crooked wood beams, cream-colored plaster, steep roof enhanced by gabled windows, and blue windowboxes spilling over with pink geraniums. The home is even more incredible inside—a virtual fantasy of flowers. Every nook and cranny is highlighted by huge, exquisitely arranged bouquets of fragrant fresh flowers. In addition, an unbelievable assortment of dried flowers, cleverly tied with pretty ribbons, hangs from the rough-hewn beamed ceilings, creating a whimsical canopy of color. All the flowers come from the garden and are dried and arranged by Elizabeth and her three daughters. Each of the cozy bedrooms has its own personality and shows Elizabeth's loving hand and artistic flair. There are antique accents in each of the bedrooms and, of course, flowers, flowers, flowers. Best of all are the owners whose happy nature permeates their little inn—the entire family opens their hearts to you in an unsurpassed welcome. I should not close without mentioning the breakfast—no, I will leave that as a surprise. *Directions:* From the A13 (Rouen to Caen) take the Lisieux exit. From Lisieux go north on D579 for about 5 km to Ouilly-le-Vicomte where you turn right on D98 signposted to Saint Philbert. Go about 4 km, then turn right on D284. The farm is on the first road on your left.

LA FERME DES POIRIERS ROSES
Hosts: Elizabeth & Jacques Lecorneur
14130 Saint Philbert des Champs, France
Tel: 02.31.64.72.14, Fax: 02.31.64.19.55
7 rooms, Double: 450F–600F
No table d'hôte
Open all year, Some English spoken
Region: Normandy, Michelin Map 231
www.karenbrown.com/france/lafermedespoiriersroses.html

Old mills are almost always extremely appealing, and the pretty, 17th-century Le Petit Moulin du Rouvre is no exception. The picturesque stone building with steeply pitched, dark slate roof nestles in a lush grassy garden next to a small mill pond that is backdropped by a dense green forest. You enter directly into the dining room which is as cozy as can be with a cradle in front of a large fireplace. Stone walls, tiled floors, country-French table and chairs in the middle of the room, a wonderful antique armoire, and colorful plates on the walls make the room very warm and appealing. An adjacent parlor, with beamed ceiling and open fireplace, is somewhat more formally decorated and has windows opening onto the pond. There are four bedrooms which are quite small and basic in decor, but immaculately clean. The choice bedroom is Les Amis, also referred to as Marine, decorated in blues and with an opening where you can look below and see the old water wheel. *Directions:* From Rennes take N137 for 40 km north towards Saint Malo. Take the Saint Pierre de Plesguen exit, then take the D10 towards Lanhelin. Before you reach Lanhelin, you see the road leading to Le Petit Moulin du Rouvre well signposted on the right side of the road. (Along the way you will see another bed and breakfast sign with another name.)

LE PETIT MOULIN DU ROUVRE (Gîtes de France)
Hostess: Annie Michel
35720 Saint Pierre de Plesguen, France
Tel: 02.99.73.85.84, Fax: 02.99.73.71.06
4 rooms, Double: 380F
No table d'hôte
Closed Nov, Very little English spoken
Region: Brittany, Michelin Map 230
www.karenbrown.com/france/lepetitmoulindurouvre.html

The Château de Roussillon is an old fortified castle, partially in ruins, perched on a rock outcrop high above a deep valley. The existing castle and towers date from the 13th and 15th centuries, but were built on the remains of a far more ancient fortress. Madame Hourriez offers extremely romantic accommodation in the ancient tower chapel. The large guestroom has a private bath and an independent entrance off the upper stone courtyard. A high stone-vaulted ceiling and exposed stone walls lend a very medieval feeling to this spacious room furnished entirely in dark-wood antiques, Oriental rugs, and tapestry wall hangings. A comfortable double bed is found near a window, set deep into the thick rock wall, offering a spectacular view over the valley below. A cozy fireplace corner beckons in the evenings or on cool autumn afternoons. Madame brings breakfast every morning to the room or to the outdoor table and chairs in the courtyard garden. For longer stays, Madame Hourriez has an equally picturesque, fully equipped apartment for up to six people. *Directions:* Saint Pierre Lafeuille is located about 8 km north of Cahors. Take N20 towards Paris and, once in the village of Saint Pierre, look for a sign pointing to the right for Château de Roussillon.

CHÂTEAU DE ROUSSILLON (Gîtes de France)
Hostess: Marcelle Hourriez
Saint Pierre Lafeuille
46090 Cahors, France
Tel: 05.65.36.87.05, Fax: 05.65.36.82.34
1 room, Double: 450F
No table d'hôte
Open Apr to Nov, Very little English spoken
Region: Lot, Michelin Map 235
www.karenbrown.com/france/chateauderoussillon.html

Far off the beaten path, Le Moulinage Chabriol is a bed and breakfast made in heaven for those who enjoy walking through quiet woodlands with only the song of the birds and the music of rushing water to interrupt the absolute quiet. Lize and Edouard de Lang wearied of their demanding careers in Holland and moved to France to enjoy a less harried life. They discovered a wonderful 18th-century silk mill high in the hills, nestled on the banks of the rushing La Glueyre river, which they renovated and remodeled to accommodate six guestrooms, five of which have a stunning view of the river below. The rooms are fairly small, but big enough for twin beds (which can be joined to make kings), a writing desk, and a chair. There is nothing contrived or "country-cozy" here—although there are some antiques used as accents, there is a pleasing austerity to the decor, with freshly painted white walls, modern blue chairs, and track lighting. Handsomely displayed on the walls is a museum-quality exhibit of very old photographs of men and women working in the silk factory. The terraced gardens surrounding the home are exceptionally beautiful. *Directions:* Leave the A7 at the Loriol exit (just south of Valence). Cross the Rhône, following signs to La Voulte, take D120 to St-Sauveur de Montagut, then D102 toward Albon. Stay on the D102. In 20 minutes (15 km) you will see the blue "Chabriol" sign on your left.

LE MOULINAGE CHABRIOL
Hosts: Lize & Edouard de Lang
Chabriol Bas
07190 Saint Pierreville, France
Tel: 04.75.66.62.08, Fax: 04.75.66.65.99
E-mail: chabriol@aol.com
6 rooms, Double: 350F
No table d'hôte
Open all year
Very good English spoken
Region: Rhône Valley, Michelin Map 244

Hilary and Tony Prime decided to make a change from their hectic professional lives in London where Tony was a newspaper photographer and Hilary was a television announcer. While visiting friends in Aubeterre, they saw and fell in love with La Sauzade, a handsome 18th-century stone manor set in 6 acres of gardens. The house is bright and cheerful with tall windows letting in the sun. There is a light, airy dining room where both Hilary and Tony are on hand with plenty of information about what to see and do in the surrounding area. A fabulous old wooden spiral staircase winds up to three guestrooms, which are homey and comfortable. In the front of the manor is a large swimming pool, a welcome respite on a hot day after sightseeing. Even if you speak French, it might be a relief to slip back into English again for a few days and not have to tax your vocabulary skills. *Directions:* Saint Romain is located 95 km northeast of Bordeaux. Take the D2 east from Chalais. Just before Aubeterre, when the road forks, turn left on D10 (signposted Montmoreau). La Sauzade is about 1 km along on the left side of the road.

LA SAUZADE
Hosts: Hilary & Tony Prime
16210 Saint Romain, France
Tel & fax: 05.45.98.63.93
3 rooms, Double: 500F–550F
Table d'hôte: 140F per person, includes wine
Open all year
Fluent English spoken
Region: Atlantic Coast, Michelin Map 233
www.karenbrown.com/france/lasauzade.html

The Auberge du Moulin de Labique sits on the rise of a hill overlooking a little creek that flows into a picture-perfect pond with lazily swimming ducks. Hélène and François Boulet-Passebon, the gracious, hard-working owners, operate the property as a farm, bed and breakfast, and restaurant where Hélène is the chef. The oldest part of their beige-stone home dates back to the 15th century. The building is typical of the area except for an amazing, two-story, columned verandah which stretches across the front, giving the effect of an ante-bellum mansion. No one can remember who added such a fanciful embellishment, but it is very old. One of the guestrooms is in the main house while the remainder are found in the old stone hay barn above the restaurant. The bedrooms are attractively decorated with pretty wallpapers, excellent country antiques, and color-coordinating fabrics—the front-facing bedroom is particularly enticing, with cheerful flower-sprigged wallpaper. In the meadow behind the house is a swimming pool. Horses frolic in a nearby field—they are beauties as François specializes in breeding fine horses (riding can be arranged). *Directions:* From Périgueux go south on N21 to Bergerac. From Bergerac take the N21 south to Castillonnès, the D2 east to Villeréral, then south towards Monflanquin for 2 km. Turn right on the D153 for 2 km to Born and south towards Saint Vivien for 2 km. Auberge du Moulin de Labique is on your left, before Saint Vivien.

AUBERGE DU MOULIN DE LABIQUE (Gîtes de France)
Hosts: Hélène & François Boulet-Passebon
Saint Vivien /Saint Eutrope de Born
47210 Villeréral, France
Tel: 05.53.01.63.90, Fax: 05.53.01.73.17
E-mail: moulin-de-labique@wanadoo.fr
6 rooms, Double: 500F–780F
Table d'hôte Nov to May, Restaurant open rest of year
Open all year, reservations required, Credit cards: VS
Good English spoken
Region: Aquitaine, Michelin Map 235
www.karenbrown.com/france/aubergedumoulin.html

The flower-filled medieval village of Salers is perched on a high point in the mountainous region of central France. Officially classified as one of the prettiest villages in France, it is a picturesque jumble of quaint, cottage-style houses and shops, all built from regional gray stone and with slate roofs. Hosts Claudine and Philippe Prudent offer travelers comfortable and practical accommodation in a separate wing of their historic house. Bedrooms are all similar in decor, featuring country-style beds, tables, and chairs and small alcoves with shower, washbasin, and WC. Exposed ceiling beams and dormer windows add character to the functional rooms. Guest quarters are accessed through a peaceful green garden with a magnificent view over the surrounding hills and valleys. Breakfast is served here in this tranquil, natural setting or, if preferred, in guest bedrooms. *Directions:* Salers is located approximately 35 km north of Aurillac. Take the N122 north from Figeac to Aurillac, then D922 north towards Mauriac on a winding, hilly road, turning right onto D680 towards Salers. Travel through the village on narrow cobblestone streets all the way to the central square. Turn left down the Rue des Nobles and look for a Chambres d'Hôtes sign marking the Prudents' house.

CHEZ PRUDENT (Gîtes de France)
Hosts: Claudine & Philippe Prudent
Rue des Nobles
15410 Salers, France
Tel: 04.71.40.75.36, Fax: none
6 rooms, Double: 240F
No table d'hôte
Open all year, Some English spoken
Region: Auvergne, Michelin Map 239

The Maison Dominxenea, which shares the same charming owners with the Hôtel Arraya in Sare, is so special that you will never want to leave. Located about a kilometer from the center of Sare (designated one of France's prettiest villages), the bed and breakfast is a picture-perfect, 16th-century cottage with cute red picket fence in front and red shutters accenting a white façade. Your enter into a cozy parlor dominated by a large fireplace. Just beyond is a second lounge that looks out onto a back garden with a lush lawn stretching back to 300 rose bushes. In the garden is a flagstone terrace, a favorite spot for guests to lounge and enjoy the idyllic scene. A handsome, centuries-old, spiral wooden staircase leads from the front parlor up to the three bedrooms, each of which is individually decorated with great taste and abounds with antiques. Fresh bouquets of flowers lend the final note of perfection. Two of the guestrooms (which are slightly more expensive) are extremely spacious. In the morning freshly baked croissants, rolls, and homemade jams are left in the pantry so guests can enjoy breakfast at their leisure. For dinner, stroll to the Hôtel Arraya where the meals are absolutely fantastic. When making reservations, since the telephone and fax numbers are the same as at the Hôtel Arraya, be *sure* to indicate whether you want a room at the hotel or the bed and breakfast. *Directions*: Leave the A63 at Saint Jean de Luz (Nord, exit 3). Take the D918 through Ascain to Sare. Go to the Hôtel Arraya in the center of the village and they will direct you to their bed and breakfast.

MAISON DOMINXENEA   New
Hosts: Laurence & Jean Baptiste Fagoaga
Quartier Ihalar
64310 Sare, France
Tel: 05.59.54.20.46, Fax: 05.59.54.27.04
3 rooms, Double: 300F–350F
No table d'hôte, restaurant at Hôtel Arraya
Open mid-Mar to mid-Nov, Very good English spoken
Region: Basque, Michelin Map 234

Near the Spanish border, the rolling green foothills of the Pyrenees are filled with picture-book villages, including Sare. Here you find an outstanding bed and breakfast, the Olhabidea. Use this perfect hideaway as your base to explore this enticing area and also to sample a little night life in the resorts of Biarritz and Saint Jean de Luz. This lovingly restored farmhouse captures the tradition and rustic flavor of the Basque region. You cannot help being captivated by the delightful ambiance of this charming home—an old wooden settle beside the fireplace whose mantle is trimmed with fabric, a rustic polished table laid with blue-and-white dishes, bouquets of fresh flowers, and comfortable sofas. The snug farmhouse atmosphere is further enhanced by the Basque blue-and-white color scheme and the polished flagstone floor set beneath the low, beamed ceiling. Every spacious bedroom has its own bathroom. A delicious breakfast is the only meal served by the effervescent Anne Marie. For dinner, guests often sample traditional Basque fare at the Hotel Arraya in Sare, owned by Anne Marie's sister-in-law. The hotel is a handy place for asking directions if you have difficulty finding Olhabidea. *Directions:* Exit the N2 autoroute at junction 3 signposted Saint Jean de Luz (Nord). Take the D918 through Ascain to Saint Pée sous Nivelle and the D3 towards Sare. After several kilometers (2 km before Sare) turn left when you see a small old church on the right. The bed and breakfast is signposted from here.

OLHABIDEA (Gîtes de France)
Hosts: Anne Marie & Jean Fagoag
64310 Sare, France
Tel: 05.59.54.21.85, Fax: 05.59.47.50.41
3 rooms, Double: 350F–400F
No table d'hôte
Open all year
No English spoken
Region: Pyrénées-Atlantiques, Michelin Map 234
www.karenbrown.com/france/olhabidea.html

If you want a sensational place to stay in the Dordogne, conveniently close to the popular tourist spots of Sarlat and Les Eyzies, look no further—La Métairie Haute is about as close to perfection as you will ever find. From the highway, a road weaves through the forest to emerge into a large, open meadow of pristine beauty, dominated by a fairy-tale manor made of lovely creamy-beige stone. A sturdy square tower joins two wings, which in days of old were separate houses, the oldest dating back to at least the 15th century. Manicured terraced lawns and flowers embrace the house, which was purchased in 1991 by your exceptionally charming hosts, Martine and Michel (both of whom speak excellent English). Happily, La Métairie is as pretty inside as out and exudes tremendous love and caring. When I arrived one early morning in May, guests were enjoying a beautifully presented, delicious-looking breakfast. Fresh roses decorated the lovely wooden dining table and blazing logs in a huge fireplace took the chill from the room, creating a mood of cozy comfort. Throughout the house, everything is picture-perfect, down to the smallest detail. All the bedrooms are beautiful and have the bonus of fabulous bathrooms. *Directions*: From Sarlat, take D47 toward Les Eyzies. After about 6 km (just before you come to the well-marked turnoff for Puymartin) turn left at the sign for La Métairie Haute. Go on for a little more than 3 km until you come to another sign for La Métairie Haute. Turn left and continue to the manor house.

LA MÉTAIRIE HAUTE   New
Hosts: Martine & Michel Pinard Legry
Lasserre, 24200 Sarlat, France
Tel: 05.53.30.31.17, Fax: 05.53.59.62.66
5 rooms, Double: 400F–500F
No table d'hôte
Open all year
Very good English spoken
Region: Dordogne, Michelin Map 233

At Le Prieuré des Granges, a handsome manor set in the hills above the Loire and the town of Savonnières in 5.5 landscaped acres, Eric offers excellence in accommodation and a genuine, personal welcome. There are two salons, one where guests of multiple nights can make themselves at home, the other a lovely room where guests congregate after breakfast and Eric helps plan their explorations. At the front of the house on the first level are three wonderful guestrooms, each with its own sitting area just outside its entry, nestled amongst greenery. Du Bellay, attractive in colors of soft orange, has a lavish bathroom and separate toilet; Ronsard, in shades of blue, has a canopied bed, a tapestry rug on a weathered tile floor, and a marvelous bread oven on the wall; Rabelais, in reds, golds, and blues, has a handsome canopy and a dramatic goat-fur cover for the bed. You enter the one suite, La Fontaine, off the garden level then climb up to a beautiful large room with two draped windows enjoying glorious views of the garden. Off the main room are a separate room with twin beds and an enormous bathroom. Off the back stairs are Flaubert, in greens and red-floral, and blue-and-cream Balzac with its own long terrace. Breakfast is served at one large table in a room just off the entry, warmed by a small wood-burning stove. *Directions:* Take the D7 to Villandry. On the east side of town, turn south on the D121 in the direction of Druyé. At the top of the hill the road splits—take the left-hand fork, signed Chambre d'Hôte. Le Prieuré des Granges is on the left.

LE PRIEURÉ DES GRANGES   **New**
Host: Eric Salmon
15, Rue des Fontaines, Route de Ballan-Mire
37510 Savonnières, France
Tel: 02.47.50.09.67, Fax: 02.47.50.06.43
E-mail: salmon.eric@wanadoo.fr
6 rooms, Double: 420F to 580F
No table d'hôte
Open Mar to Nov, Good English spoken
Region: Loire Valley, Michelin Map 232

Le Prieuré Sainte Anne is a peaceful bed and breakfast, offering a warm welcome in a tranquil, appealing setting. This 15th-century cottage recalls the days of Joan of Arc with its low, beamed ceilings and exposed stone walls. Madame Caré is a motherly hostess who obviously takes great pleasure in welcoming guests to her charming, ivy-covered home. Her well-tended garden provides fresh-flower arrangements and her rooms are furnished in highly polished family antiques. She offers one suite of two bedrooms sharing a simple bathroom, accessed by its own staircase. The price is reasonable and it is ideal for a family of three or four. The two bedrooms are large, one having a queen bed and the other twins. The rooms have handsome (non-functioning) stone fireplaces, weathered tiled floors, and small-paned, leaded-glass windows that look out over the peaceful courtyard and secret garden. A breakfast of breads, jams, and beverage is offered downstairs at a handsome trestle table in a room next to Madame's own private quarters. *Directions:* Savonnières is located about 11 km southwest of Tours on the south bank of the Loire via D7 in the direction of Villandry. On the eastern edge of town, leave the river, turning up the hill in the direction of Ballon, and then turn immediately right on Rue Chaude, signposted Le Prieuré Sainte-Anne. A Chambre d'Hôte sign identifies Madame Caré's wood-gated driveway. (Do not be confused by the sign to the Prieuré, another bed and breakfast farther up the hill.)

LE PRIEURÉ SAINTE-ANNE (Gîtes de France)
Hostess: Lucette Caré
10, Rue Chaude, Joué Les Tours
37510 Savonnières, France
Tel: 02.47.50.03.26, Fax: none
1 suite, Double: 320F (2-night minimum)
No table d'hôte
Open all year
No English spoken
Region: Loire Valley, Michelin Map 232
www.karenbrown.com/france/leprieuresainteanne.html

Saint Jean is a most attractive, two-story, buff-colored home with red-tiled roof and blue shutters, a style typical of this beautiful region of Provence. This appealing bed and breakfast, perfect for several days' exploration of Provence, has an ideal setting on a small rise of hill, a site continuously occupied since the 10th century when a monastery was built here. Many tourist sites are easily reached in less than one hour from Saint Jean. With her children growing older, the extremely gracious Gisele Augier decided to convert some of the space in her large home into a bed and breakfast. She now has an attractively decorated lounge exclusively for the use of guests with game tables, television, and comfortable chairs, plus three bedrooms, each with a private entrance. The immaculately kept bedrooms are very tastefully decorated with pretty color-coordinated fabrics and a few pieces of antique furniture. My favorite (the yellow bedroom) costs slightly more, but has its own little terrace overlooking the garden. Gisele prepares delicious breakfasts that include one "surprise" each day. Behind the house is a peaceful little park with lily ponds and a lush lawn. Tall trees through which you can see vineyards edge the property. There is also a large swimming pool set on a terrace overlooking a field of grapes. *Directions:* From the A7 (Lyon to Aix en Provence) exit at Orange and continue on N977 towards Vaison La Romaine. At the Seguret crossroads turn right on D88 towards Seguret. Go 800 meters then turn left: Saint Jean is the second house on the left.

SAINT JEAN (Gîtes de France)
Hostess: Gisele Augier
84110 Seguret, France
Tel: 04.90.46.91.76, Fax: 04.90.46.83.88
E-mail: marc.aguier@wanadoo.fr
3 rooms, Double: 490F–570F
No table d'hôte
Open all year, Little English spoken
Region: Provence, Michelin Map 245
www.karenbrown.com/france/saintjean.html

Luckily, a reader who lives in Paris shared her discovery of Le Clos des Tourelles with us and now we can pass on to you this superb find. Le Clos des Tourelles is nestled in a 17-hectare park, right in the center of Sennecey-Le-Grand. The heritage of the estate dates back to the 12th century. Today there are three buildings on the property, one being a beautiful small château with a gray-slate mansard roof. This is where you find the guestrooms—and what beauties they are, all totally furnished with fine antiques enhanced by lovely fabrics. The owner, Madame Derudder, personally decorated each one with great skill and loving care—every tiny detail is perfect. Another building is a charming timbered house, accented by two jaunty towers and a galleried walkway overhanging the terrace below. Inside is a cozy kitchen where dinner is served when there are only a few guests dining. If there are more than eight persons choosing table d'hôte, you are in for a real treat! In that case, dinner is served in a stunning medieval tower at a long table magnificently set with fine linens and crystal in front of an enormous stone fireplace. As an added bonus, there is a swimming pool in the garden. *Directions:* Take the A6 south from Beaune in the direction of Lyon. Take the Chalon-sur-Saone exit and go south on N6 to Sennecey-Le-Grand. In the middle of the village, turn to your right, following the signs to Le Clos des Tourelles.

LE CLOS DES TOURELLES (Gîtes de France)
Hostess: Madame Laurence Derudder
71240 Sennecey-Le-Grand, France
Tel: 03.85.44.83.95, Fax: 03.85.44.90.18
8 rooms, Double: 400F–840F
Table d'hôte: 200F per person
Open all year
Little English spoken
Region: Burgundy, Michelin Map 243

The Jezequel family offers old-fashioned hospitality and delicious farm-fresh meals at the quaint Ferme Auberge de Sepvret. Their 300-year-old home is covered with ivy and surrounded by a pretty, flower-filled garden. Farm-style meals are served in the intimate and homelike dining room furnished with round wooden tables adorned with bouquets of fresh flowers and a cheerful selection of tablecloths. Traditional home-cooked fare features regional specialties such as *farci poitevin*, a type of soufflé made from garden greens (spinach, cabbage, parsley, and sorrel), eggs, sour cream, and spices. Simple country charm is felt throughout the house and in the guest bedrooms which are furnished with brass beds, old armoires, and flowered wallpapers. Large windows open out to the back garden, letting in plenty of light and fresh air. Days usually begin with a romantic and peaceful breakfast enjoyed outdoors at a table set under the trees. *Directions:* Sepvret is located about 45 km southwest of Poitiers. Take N10 towards Angoulême for 2 km, then turn off onto N11 (which later becomes D150) and travel in the direction of Niort, La Rochelle, and Saintes. Turn right after about 40 km onto D108 to Sepvret. Once in the village, follow signs for Chambres d'Hôtes and Ferme Auberge which lead to the Jezequels' home.

FERME AUBERGE DE SEPVRET (Gîtes de France)
Hosts: Françoise & Claude Jezequel
Sepvret
79120 Lezay, France
Tel: 05.49.07.33.73, Fax: none
3 rooms, Double: 220F
Table d'hôte: 70F per person
Open all year
Very little English spoken
Region: Atlantic Coast, Michelin Map 233

Le Petit Manoir, a typical two-story, stone, Normandy-style home with red-tiled roof, is flanked on two sides by farm buildings and fronted by a stone wall. From the moment you drive into the courtyard, you notice that everything is as neat as a new pin. The characterful, centuries-old stone house is brightened with climbing roses, flowerboxes at the windows, pots of geraniums, and a circular flower bed. Inside, Annick's good housekeeping is again evident, for everything is spotlessly clean and tidy. Annick's bed and breakfast occupies one wing of the house. On the ground floor is a small breakfast room—although guests usually eat outside when the weather is warm. An exterior staircase leads to two small, meticulously kept bedrooms which, although simple in decor, are very nice, with contemporary furnishings, sweet floral-pattern wallpaper, and private bathrooms. The bedrooms are almost identical, but the one facing the back has a special surprise—from the window you see cornfields stretching off to the distant shoreline, with Mont Saint Michel on the horizon. For budget accommodation, Le Petit Manoir offers a warm welcome and far more class and comfort than usually found at this price. *Directions:* From Caen head southwest on N175. Go through Avranches and continue on the N175 for about 12 km. Turn right at Servon and go straight into the village. When the street ends, turn right: Le Petit Manoir is down the road on the left.

LE PETIT MANOIR
Hosts: Annick & Jean Gédouin
Il Rue de la Pierre du Tertre
50170 Servon, France
Tel: 02.33 60.03.44, Fax: 02.33.60.17.79
2 rooms, Double: 220F
No table d'hôte
Open all year
Very little English spoken
Region: Normandy, Michelin Map 231

Le Chaufourg is truly a dream—absolute perfection. Georges Dambier has created an exquisite work of art from what was originally a rustic 18th-century farmhouse that has been in his family "forever." The task of renovation was formidable, but all the ingredients were there: the house, built of beautiful soft-yellow stone, already had charm and its location on a bend of the Isle river is idyllic. Although strategically located in the heart of the Dordogne and conveniently near access roads to all the major sights of interest, once within the gates leading to the romantic front courtyard, one feels insulated from the real world. The exterior of the house is like a fairy-tale cottage with its white-shuttered doors and windows laced with ivy and surrounded by masses of colorful flower gardens. Inside, the magic continues. Each guestroom is entirely different, yet each has the same mood of quiet, country elegance, with natural stucco walls of warm honey-beige, stunning antiques, and tones of soft whites and creams. You find nothing stiff or intimidating—just the elegant harmony of country comfort created by an artist. Georges Dambier adds the final ingredient—the warmth of genuine hospitality. Another plus— superb meals are served in Le Chaufourg's exquisite restaurant. *Directions:* From Périgueux take N89 southwest in the direction of Bordeaux for about 32 km to Sourzac (about 3 km before Mussidan). You see the entrance to Le Chaufourg on the right side of the road.

LE CHAUFOURG EN PÉRIGORD
Host: Georges Dambier
24400 Sourzac, France
Tel: 05.53.81.01.56, Fax: 05.53.82.94.87
E-mail: chaufourg.hotel@wanadoo.fr
9 rooms, Double: 1,040F–1,720F
2-night min, Children over 10
Restaurant, Open Apr to Nov (by reservation only)
Credit cards: all major, Very good English spoken
Region: Dordogne, Michelin Map 233
www.karenbrown.com/france/lechaufourgenperigord.html

The Mas de Champelon, in the heart of the Côtes du Rhône region of Provence, offers outstanding value for travelers on a tight budget. You can stay here in a charming old farmhouse with great comfort and gracious hosts without sacrificing one iota of quality. A gate on the main road opens onto the courtyard of the handsome stone farmhouse, which has been handed down through several generations of Christiane's family. When she inherited it, it was in need of total renovation to be livable, so her talented husband, Michael, completely rebuilt it with his own labor. Today the home is a real delight. The mellow-stone house opens onto a terrace facing a lovely garden beyond which stretch fields of grapes. There are four pleasant guestrooms. Although not especially large, each is individually decorated and has a fresh, pretty look with color-coordinating provincial-print fabric used for the bedspreads and the curtains. Dinner is served family-style at one big table in an attractive dining room where a large fireplace and baskets hanging from the beamed ceiling add a charming country flavor. *Directions:* Suze La Rousse is about 21 km north of Orange. Take the A7 and exit at Bollène (exit 18), following directions for Suze La Rousse. Leave Suze La Rousse on the D59 toward Saint Paul Trois Château, but turn right almost immediately onto a small country road (CD117) toward La Baume de Transit. Soon you will see the gate to the Mas de Champelon on your right.

MAS DE CHAMPELON
Hosts: Christiane & Michael Zebbar
Hameau de Saint Turquois
26790 Suze La Rousse, France
Tel: 04.75.98.81.95, Fax: none
4 rooms, Double: 250F
Table d'hôte: 95F per person
Open Apr 4 to Sep 3
Very little English spoken
Region: Provence, Michelin Map 245

If you want to explore the Côte d'Azur and feel like you are staying with friends from home, Le Mas du Soleil makes an ideal choice for accommodation. Your gracious hosts, Barbara and Curt Wible, extend a genuine welcome, opening not only their home but also their hearts to those who visit. Barbara and Curt both had successful careers in the United States, but the thought of leaving their frantic lifestyle, taking early retirement, and moving to France became ever more attractive—so they just did it! Soon after their move they found the perfect property high in the hills above Nice, just outside the picturesque village of Tourrettes-sur-Loup. Luckily, Curt is a skilled craftsman and Barbara has a real gift with flowers, so between them they have created a beautiful garden and three deluxe guestrooms with private entrance and private bath. From the front of the house, facing the main road, you can catch a glimpse of the sea, but I prefer the gorgeous back garden with its Olympic-sized swimming pool, shaded terrace, wide expanse of lush lawn, and romantic view up to the magnificent layers of densely wooded hills. *Directions:* From Nice, take the A8 west and exit at Cagnes-sur-Mer (exit 48). Follow signs to Vence then when the road splits, take the left branch of the road signposted Tourrettes-sur-Loup. Just before you arrive in Tourrettes-sur-Loup, Le Mas du Soleil is on you right with two stone pillars marking the gate. Watch for the street number 641.

LE MAS DU SOLEIL   **New**
Hosts: Barbara & Curt Wible
641, Route de Vence
06140 Tourrettes-sur-Loup, France
Tel: 04.93.24.15.23, Fax: 04.93.24.16.73
E-mail: bwible@wanadoo.fr
3 rooms, Double: 600F
No table d'hôte
Open May to Oct, 2-night minimum
Fluent English spoken
Region: Provence, Michelin Map 245

Overlooking the scenic River Loire and the pastoral valley beyond, on the site where Richard the Lionheart installed his troops at the end of the 12th century, stands the stately Château de la Voûte. Termed a bed and breakfast by the owners, the quality of its comfort and the elegance of its furnishings rival some of France's loveliest châteaux. It was a treat to explore each of the five bedrooms, all with private bath, as they are individual and outstanding in their decor, having received the artful attention of both Véronique and Richard. Gorgeous antiques, handsome fabrics, lovely carpets, and original art are beautifully coordinated. Although there are no public rooms available to guests, the bedrooms have comfortable seating areas and excellent lighting. A breakfast feast is served on the garden terrace or in the bedrooms before large windows whose shutters open up to the fresh morning air. In the evening it is an enjoyable walk down the garden path and a short stroll along the village street to an outstanding country restaurant, Le Cheval Blanc. Charming, convenient, and reasonably priced, Le Cheval Blanc is a welcome bonus as the Château de la Voûte does not serve meals other than breakfast. (Chef Michel Coyault, tel: 02.54.72.58.22, closed Monday nights.) *Directions:* From Tours, take the N10 north to Vendôme and then travel west on the D917 to the village of Troo.

CHÂTEAU DE LA VOÛTE
Hosts: Véronique & Richard Provenzano
41800 Troo, France
Tel & fax: 02.54.72.52.52
E-mail: chatlavout@aol.com
5 rooms, Double: 490F–600F
No table d'hôte
Open all year, Some English spoken
Region: Loire Valley, Michelin Map 238
www.karenbrown.com/france/chateaudelavoute.html

Except for its setting of great natural beauty, Les Volets Bleus does not immediately appear special—just a small, modern, ochre house with cheerful blue shutters. But don't be put off by first impressions: the five guestrooms are found in a separate, centuries-old stone farmhouse of great charm. Although simple, this bed and breakfast is exceptionally inviting, the hospitality outstanding, and the scenery breathtaking. The bedrooms and bathrooms are fairly small but very attractive, extremely comfortable, decorated with taste, and as clean as new pennies. Three of the rooms have doors opening onto private terraces. Clever Pilar has thought of every detail to make her guests comfortable and her genuine warmth and happy disposition permeate the air, making visitors feel like friends of the family. She and her husband Carlo share in the cooking. The meals are delicious, with most of the produce coming from the garden. If you are traveling with children, Les Volets Bleus would make an excellent accommodation choice—little ones are wholeheartedly welcomed and there are chickens, donkeys, and even a wooded area with a tree house. *Directions*: Exit the A7 at Montélimar Sud. Follow white signs to Dieulefit. In Dieulefit, turn north on D538 toward Bourdeaux. Before you reach Bourdeaux, take a small road on your left marked to Truinas. Before Truinas, Les Volets Bleus is signposted on your right.

LES VOLETS BLEUS
Hosts: Pilar & Carlo Fortunato
26460 Truinas, France
Tel: 04.75.53.38.48, Fax: 04.75.53.49.02
E-mail: lesvolets@aol.com
5 rooms, Double: 300F
Table d'hôte: 125F per person
Open all year
Good English spoken
Region: Provence-Drôme, Michelin Map 245

The ancient Roman town of Vaison La Romaine is found in a hilly, wooded setting in northern Provence. Just outside of town on a high point affording panoramic views of the surrounding mountains and plains, the Delesses' 150-year-old stone house offers a refined haven for travelers. The bedroom, well soundproofed by thick old stone walls, is accessible from an independent entrance. French doors lead to an intimate terrace overlooking a restful view of fields and distant hills. The room is tastefully decorated and very comfortable, with a writing table and bookcase stocked for guests' enjoyment. Monsieur and Madame are both teachers, specializing in French and English respectively, so communication is no problem and convivial breakfasts are enjoyed together in their cozy beamed breakfast room or outside in the tranquil front courtyard. A pool has been added since our visit. *Directions:* Vaison La Romaine is about 18 km north of Carpentras via D938. If coming from Avignon, follow signs to Orange, and then for Vaison La Romaine. Upon entering the town, go towards the Super U supermarket. At the traffic circle, follow sign to Nyons. At the second traffic circle, take the left and follow the road between the school and the stadium, then turn right, then left again into Chemin de l'Ioou. The Delesses' driveway is on the right and is marked with a Chambres d'Hôtes sign.

CHEZ DELESSE (Gîtes de France)
Hosts: François & Claude Delesse
Chemin de l'Ioou
Le Brusquet, 84110 Vaison La Romaine, France
Tel & fax: 04.90.36.38.38
1 room, Double: 300F, 1 Suite: 500F
No table d'hôte
Open all year, Very good English spoken
Region: Provence, Michelin Maps 245, 246
www.karenbrown.com/france/chezdelesse.html

Vaison La Romaine, an unspoiled fortified village rising steeply from the banks of the Ouveze river, has a superb bed and breakfast owned by the Verdier family. Jean, an architect, and Aude, his pretty wife, moved from Paris to this ancient walled city in 1975 and worked together to transform the ruins of what was once a part of the bishop's palace into a gracious home for themselves and their three sons. There are four guest bedrooms with their own charmingly decorated lounge and a private entrance to the street. Of the guestrooms, my favorites are the twin-bedded rooms which have more of an antique ambiance than the double-bedded room with its bit of an art-deco feel. Aude serves breakfast on an enticing terrace snuggled amongst the rooftops or, when the weather is chilly, in the family dining room. Although Aude and Jean speak only a smattering of English, their absolutely genuine warmth will guarantee a very special stay in this highly recommended bed and breakfast. *Directions:* Vaison La Romaine is located 45 km northeast of Avignon. When you reach the town of Vaison La Romaine, cross the river and climb the narrow road to the Ville Médiévale. L'Évêché is on the right side of the main street, Rue de l'Évêché.

L'ÉVÊCHÉ   (Gîtes de France)
Hosts: Aude & Jean Loup Verdier
Rue de l'Évêché, Ville Médiévale
84110 Vaison La Romaine, France
Tel: 04.90.36.13.46, Fax: 04.90.36.32.43
E-mail: eveche@aol.com
4 rooms, Double: 400F–440F
No table d'hôte
Open all year, Very little English spoken
Region: Provence, Michelin Maps 245, 246
www.karenbrown.com/france/leveche.html

La Croix du Grès is an especially beautiful bed and breakfast. Your heart will be won the minute you drive up to this enchanting, honey-toned stone house accentuated by fresh white trim, softened with greenery, and cheerfully accented by a multitude of colorful plants. This charming farmhouse has a whimsical feeling with its jumble of rooflines and jutting chimneys. Large meadows surround the home and a beautiful, stone-enclosed swimming pool nestles in the back garden. Monsieur Leroy, the owner, was away when we visited, but from the personal experience of our "reader on the road" who discovered this jewel for us, he is delightfully gracious and extremely helpful—guiding his guests to interesting places and helping them to plan fantastic walks. We were disappointed to have missed him but, luckily, a guest (who loved his accommodations) took heed of our plight and kindly showed us around the splendid property. There are three bedrooms and two suites (each with a kitchenette, dining room, and parlor). Privacy is insured as all the rooms and suites have their own entrance. We look forward to the pleasure of meeting Monsieur Leroy, but in the meantime, this gem is too good to pass up until a later edition. *Directions*: From the A7, take the Montelimar Sud exit. After the toll plaza, turn left, go 2 km, then turn left again toward Grignan. Keep following signs for Grignan and just before you reach Valaurie, turn right on D541—almost immediately you will see La Croix du Grès signposted on the left.

LA CROIX DU GRÈS
Host: Jacques Leroy
26230 Valaurie, France
Tel & fax: 04.75.98.51.45
E-mail: jaleroy@minitel.net
3 rooms, Double: 400F–500F, 2 suites: 570F
Table d'hôte: 100F per person
Open all year
Good English spoken
Region: Provence, Michelin Map 245

The *Lady A* is certainly not your typical bed and breakfast—it is a barge. But the quality is so high, the warmth of welcome so genuine, and the price so low that it is a pleasure to recommend it. Lisa (who's Dutch) has been in the hospitality business for a very long time. For 20 years she chartered sailboats in the Mediterranean and the Caribbean before moving to France where she and her husband refitted the *Lady A* to charter on the Burgundy canals. Nowadays the 100-foot barge moves no more but remains moored on a charming small canal in an absolutely beautiful setting—beneath Châteauneuf, an extremely picturesque walled village crowning the nearby hill. The colorful barge is lots of fun. You quickly become friends with the other guests in a house-party atmosphere. Each of the three staterooms has a private bathroom (the shower is not enclosed, but is adequate). The bedrooms (as would be expected on a boat) are just big enough for two beds (which can be made into a king-sized bed), a closet, and shelves for clothes. When not sleeping or exploring Burgundy, guests spend most of their time on the deck—a great place to enjoy a drink in the twilight and watch the action of the other boats on the waterway. *Directions:* From the A6 take the Pouilly-en-Auxois exit through Créancy to Vandenesse (D18)—*Lady A* is moored in the basin to the left of the road.

LADY A (Gîtes de France)
Hostess: Lisa Jansen Bourne
Port du Canal, Cedex 45
21320 Vandenesse-en-Auxois, France
Tel: 03.80.49.26.96, Fax: 03.80.49.27.00
3 rooms, Double: 300F
Table d'hôte: 130F per person, includes wine
Open all year, Fluent English spoken
Region: Côte d'Or, Michelin Map 243
www.karenbrown.com/france/ladya.html

Bed & Breakfast Descriptions

Villa Velleron had been abandoned for 40 years when Simone and Wim bravely bought the property. During restoration, they discovered treasures such as a beautiful stone wall no one knew existed and clues to the building's varied heritage—they found an old olive press and racks used for the processing of silk. Simone Sanders is a well-known Dutch industrial designer, so it is not surprising that there is such exceptionally artistic perfection in every detail of the house, dramatically blending old and new. There is a stunning swimming pool romantically nestled on a terrace bordered by picturesque stone walls, and an inner courtyard that simply oozes charm—potted geraniums, ivy-draped walls, fragrant roses, and lush lawn make every niche a dream. It is in this enclosed garden that guests enjoy both breakfast and dinner at small tables draped in pretty Provençal-print fabric. Although the sitting and dining rooms have a decidedly Provençal charm, each of the bedrooms follows a specific theme which varies all the way from art-deco to Oriental. Simone's husband, Wim, who is in charge of the kitchen, is also exceptionally talented. Several major magazines have featured the outstanding food, imaginative decor, and the architectural design of the Villa Velleron. *Directions:* From Carpentras take D49 south to Velleron. Villa Velleron is in the center of Velleron, down a small lane, catty-corner across the square from the post office.

VILLA VELLERON (Gîtes de France)
Hosts: Simone Sanders & Wim Visser
Rue Roquette
84740 Velleron, France
Tel: 04.90.20.12.31, Fax: 04.90.20.10.34
E-mail: villa.velleron@wanadoo.fr
6 rooms, Double: 500F–650F
Table d'hôte: 160F per person, Open Easter to Nov
Fluent English spoken, Children over 12
Region: Provence, Michelin Map 245
www.karenbrown.com/france/villavelleron.html

In French, La Maison aux Volets Bleus means The House of the Blue Shutters—indeed, the bright cobalt shutters of the Marets' charming home can be seen from far below the hilltop town of Venasque. Follow a winding road up from the plains to this ancient town which is now a haven for painters and art lovers. An old stone archway leads to the Marets' romantic walled garden and their picturesque home filled with colorful dried-flower bouquets hanging from every available rafter. The cozy living room opens onto a balcony with a sensational panoramic view. Each bedroom is unique and decorated with Martine Maret's artistic flair for harmonious colors, Provençal prints, and simple, attractive furnishings. Martine and her husband Jerome are an energetic couple with many talents who enjoy welcoming guests into their home and to their table. Plan to stay for several days to enjoy genuine hospitality and delicious meals. *Directions:* From the A7 take the Avignon North exit following signs northeast to Carpentras. From Carpentras take the D4 towards Apt for 8 km and turn to Venasque. Look for the turnoff marked Venasque to the right up a hill. Continue to the fountain square (*Place de la Fontaine*) and look for a Chambres d'Hôtes sign down the road a little to the left indicating the arched entry to the Marets' home.

LA MAISON AUX VOLETS BLEUS (*Gîtes de France*)
Hosts: Martine & Jerome Maret
Place des Bouviers
Le Village, 84210 Venasque, France
Tel: 04.90.66.03.04, Fax: 04.90.66.16.14
E-mail: voletbleu@aol.com
6 rooms, Double: 420F–500F, Suite: 780F
Table d'hôte (Mon, Wed & Sat): 135F per person
Open Mar to Nov, Good English spoken
Region: Provence, Michelin Maps 245, 246
www.karenbrown.com/france/lamaisonauxvoletsbleus.html

Domaine de Montpierreux is one of the budget entries in our guide. However, do not judge this bed and breakfast by its room rates, for this 19th-century farmhouse has great charm. A small lane leads up through the fields to the large, two-story house whose buff-colored façade is accented by white shutters. The farm is owned by the gracious Françoise and François Choné who warmly welcome guests into their home. Handsome family antiques accent the simple, yet most attractive rooms on the ground floor. At the end of the hall, a staircase spirals up through the tower to five bedrooms tucked under the steeply pitched roof. Each of the bedrooms has a cozy quality created by open beams and gabled windows. The impeccably kept rooms are simple in decor, yet attractive, with individual color schemes. On the same floor as the guestrooms, there is a lounge and game room which can be combined with a bedroom to make a family suite. Behind the house, a shaded path leads through the forest to a vineyard from which the Chonés harvest grapes and produce wine. There are also truffle grounds on the property. If you'd like to experience a working farm, you will find Domaine de Montpierreux a real winner. *Directions:* From the A6 exit at Auxerre Sud and follow the D965 in the direction of Chablis for 3 km. The lane leading to the Domaine de Montpierreux is signposted off the D965 to your right.

DOMAINE DE MONTPIERREUX (Gîtes de France)
Hosts: Françoise & François Choné
Domaine de Montpierreux
Route de Chablis, 89290 Venoy, France
Tel: 03.86.40.20.91, Fax: 03.86.40.28.00
5 rooms, Double: 280F–300F, Suite: 340F
No table d'hôte
Closed Christmas, Very little English spoken
Region: Burgundy, Michelin Map 237
www.karenbrown.com/france/domainedemontpierreux.html

In a tranquil setting of pasture, orchard, and neighboring forest, La Réserve is a beautiful amber-wash, two-story manor just a short drive from the town of Giverny, whose owners offer guests a most enthusiastic and genuine welcome. Unbelievably, the building is of new construction—with much hard work and love, Marie Lorraine and Didier built it themselves, repaired furniture, and made all the curtains. The result is a gorgeous, elegant, and wonderfully comfortable hotel with exceptional accommodation. On the ground floor you find a beautiful salon with fireplace and old pool table, a gorgeous dining room, and an adorable guestroom tucked just below the stairs looking out through large windows across to the orchards and the fields grazed by cattle. Upstairs, guestrooms under high, beamed ceilings are magnificent. Twin or queen beds are set on creaking wooden floors topped with attractive throw rugs, while large, shuttered windows open onto greenery and seem almost to frame a painting worthy of Monet. Just 45 minutes from CDG airport, this would be a convenient beginning or end to a trip. From here you can easily explore Normandy, take a day to experience Giverny, a day to visit the American Museum, and at least one day to laze in the countryside. *Directions*: Depending on the approach, either turn right past the American Museum or left past the church at the *charcuterie* and travel uphill (C3) 900 meters until you see Didier's white arrows. Turn left, follow the lane, then go left again on the drive just past the orchard.

LA RÉSERVE   **New**
Hosts: Marie Lorraine & Didier Brunet
27620 Giverny, France
Tel & fax: 02.32.21.99.09, Cellular: 06.11.25.37.44
5 rooms, Double: 480F–680F
No table d'hôte
Open Apr to Oct, in winter by reservation
Credit cards: none, No smoking
Very good English spoken
Region: Normandy, Michelin Map 237
www.karenbrown.com/france/lareserve.html

Accolades about this discovery came from a couple who has used over 30 of our recommendations and "found them always exactly as represented—and in many cases even better than described." Well, Mr. and Mrs. Doty, thank you for directing us to La Ferme—it is even better than you described! Located just south of Tournus, in a farm village just up from the River Saône, this wonderful complex is guarded by heavy doors. Framing the courtyard, the whitewashed walls of the main farmhouse are a showcase for protruding beams and exposed stone, while beautiful red tiles, weathered by the sun, add a splash of color. The five guestrooms, found up two mirroring stairways, are tucked under the steep pitch of the old roof. Low doorways, enormous beams and exposed, thick nails are evidence of the age of this charming old complex. The spotlessly modern bathrooms, excellent plumbing and lighting, and comfortable beds topped with cozy down comforters are testament to the work and attention to detail that the Stahel-Zerlauths have lavished. Their professional level of service is reflective of the finest Swiss hotels in which they both made a career for more than three decades An accomplished chef, Ruedi is also responsible for the evening meals with menus that change daily, incorporating the farm's own produce. Immaculate accommodation and incredible attention to detail make this an extremely comfortable as well as charming bed and breakfast. *Directions:* Exit the Lyon–Dijon motorway at Tournus and then take the N6 south in the direction of Mâcon. Le Villars is a little village to the east of N6.

LA FERME DU VILLARS
Hosts: Ilse & Ruedi Stahel-Zerlauth
71700 Le Villars, France
Tel: 03.85.32.51.85, Fax: 03.85.32.57.44
5 rooms, Double: 490F
Table d'hôte: à la carte
Open Apr to Nov, Credit cards: MC, VS
Fluent English spoken
Region: Burgundy, Michelin Map 243

The fairy-tale-like Château du Riau, although charmingly small, happily lacks none of the accoutrements of a proper castle. A bridge spans the ancient moat and leads through a whimsical, twin-towered keep (fashioned from bricks arranged in a fanciful diamond design) into the enclosed courtyard. Facing the courtyard, the two-story manor house with steep gray-slate roof reflects a harmonious blend of styles from the 15th, 16th, and 17th centuries. The present Baron and Baronne Durye are descendants of the original owner, Charles Papillon, a goldsmith from Moulins, who received the property from Anne de Beaujeu, daughter of King Louis XI. Although a historical monument and at times open to the public for tours, the castle is definitely a family home, occupied by the Duryes and their three sons. Reached by an impressive circular stone staircase, the bedrooms are beautifully appointed in fine antiques and all look onto a tranquil forest. My favorite, a large corner room with pretty blue-and-white wallpaper, is especially bright and cheerful. Throughout the house, family portraits and memorabilia abound. I particularly enjoyed the portrait of one portly ancestor who, it turns out, was an officer who fought in the American Revolution with Lafayette. *Directions:* From Moulins take the N7 north towards Nevers for 15 km. Just after the dual carriageway changes to two lanes, you see the lane to the château signposted to your right.

CHÂTEAU DU RIAU (Gîtes de France)
Hosts: Baron & Baronne Joseph Durye
03460 Villeneuve-sur-Allier, France
Tel: 04.70.43.34.47, Fax: 04.70.43.30.74
5 rooms, Double: 650F–750F, Apt: 800F
Table d'hôte: 200F per person, includes wine
Open Mar to Dec, Good English spoken
Region: Centre Bourbonnais, Michelin Map 238
www.karenbrown.com/france/chateauduriau.html

When Christine and Xavier Ferry bought Ferme du Château, 25 kilometers west of Reims, it looked absolutely hopeless: no water, no electricity, cows and pigs living in the house. However, with the help of family and friends, they transformed the derelict house back into a proper home. Christine and Xavier have boundless energy. He runs the farm and, when cows became unprofitable, he turned the grazing ground into an 18-hole golf course. (Energetic guests will also enjoy the tennis court on the grounds.) Christine is a busy mother, yet manages to offer four of her nicely decorated bedrooms to the public. She is also an exceptionally good chef and prepares an evening meal with advance reservation. From the front, the building looks like a farmhouse flanked by stone barns but from the rear garden with its own little stream, the house looks quite different: more like a small, turreted castle. *Directions:* From the A4 (Paris to Reims road) take the Dormans exit 21. Turn right towards Dormans, right again back over the expressway towards Villers Agron, then right at the first road which leads to the Ferme du Château.

FERME DU CHÂTEAU (Gîtes de France)
Hosts: Christine & Xavier Ferry
02130 Villers-Agron, France
Tel: 03.23.71.60.67, Fax: 03.23.69.36.54
E-mail: xavferry@club-internet.fr
4 rooms, Double: 360F–430F
Table d'hôte: 180F per person, includes wine
Open all year, Fluent English spoken
Region: Champagne, Michelin Map 237

The 13th-century Château de Villiers-Le-Mahieu fulfills any childhood fantasy to live in a fairy-tale castle. The beautifully maintained castle sits in parklike grounds, manicured to perfection, on its own little island surrounded by a moat. The main access is over a narrow bridge leading into the inner courtyard-garden, framed on three sides by the ivy-covered stone walls of the château. The Château de Villiers-Le-Mahieu is not a homey little castle where one becomes chummy with the owners, but rather a commercial operation with 26 guestrooms in the château and 11 in the garden annex. Splurge and request room 1, a grand room in the original castle, wallpapered in a handsome blue print fabric which repeats in the drapes at the three tall French windows looking out to the gardens. In the park surrounding the castle there are tennis courts and a superb swimming pool. *Directions:* Located 40 km southwest of Paris. Take the A13 west from Paris and exit south on A12 toward Dreux-Bois d'Arcy. Continue following the signs to Dreux until you come to Pontchartrain, then take D11 signposted to Thoiry. As the road leaves Thoiry, turn left on D45 toward Villiers le Mahieu and continue through the town—you will see signs to the château on the left side of the road.

CHÂTEAU DE VILLIERS-LE-MAHIEU
Host: Jean-Luc Chaufour
78770 Villiers-Le-Mahieu, France
Tel: 01.34.87.44.25, Fax: 01.34.87.44.40
37 rooms, Double: 766F–1,146F*
*Rates higher in Jul & Aug when dinner is included
Closed Christmas, Credit cards: AX, VS
Good English spoken
Region: Ile-de-France, Michelin Map 237
www.karenbrown.com/france/chateaudevilliers.html

James and Marie-Jose Hamel are an exceptionally friendly couple who take great pleasure in welcoming guests to their manor home. Originally a fortress dating from the 12th century, Le Château was rebuilt in 1450 and again in 1750 and has a colorful history. The Hamels are fond of recounting the story of their most famous visitor, Andy Rooney of *Sixty Minutes* fame. Rooney worked here as a journalist during World War II when the château was inhabited by the American Press Corps and revisited in 1984. Breakfast is served in the former press room complete with brass nameplate in English still intact on the door. A lofty ceiling, dark, pine-paneled walls, and a lovely old tile floor provide intimate surroundings to begin the day or enjoy an evening aperitif. Guest bedrooms are tastefully furnished and decorated with handsome antiques and harmonious color schemes. The rooms are found in a separate wing of the château, thus affording guests a convenient, private entry. *Directions:* Vouilly is located approximately 25 km west of Bayeux. Take D5 west to Le Molay Littry, then turn right, continuing on D5 in the direction of Isigny-sur-Mer until you reach Vouilly. Just after entering Vouilly, look for a Chambres d'Hôtes sign directing you to turn right onto a winding road—follow it to the Hamels' driveway.

LE CHÂTEAU (Gîtes de France)
Hosts: Marie-Jose & James Hamel
Vouilly, 14230 Isigny-sur-Mer, France
Tel: 02.31.22.08.59, Fax: 02.31.22.90.58
5 rooms, Double: 320F–380F
No table d'hôte, Ferme Auberge nearby
Open Mar to Dec, Credit cards: MC, VS
Very little English spoken
Region: Normandy, Michelin Map 231
www.karenbrown.com/france/lechateau.html

Nestled on the shore of Lake Geneva, the tiny walled medieval village of Yvoire is positively captivating—almost too quaint to be real. Its allure is even more captivating in summer when every available bit of land is a flower garden and every house draped with red geraniums. Making everything perfect, there is a gem of a small hotel here—the 200-year-old Hôtel du Port which absolutely oozes charm, with a stone façade almost totally covered with ivy, brown shutters, and red geraniums spilling out of windowboxes. It is just next to the dock where ferries flit in and out all day, making their circuit around the lake. The main focus of the hotel is its restaurant which has a summer dining terrace stretching to the edge of the water. Although the majority of guests come just for lunch, for a lucky few there are four sweet bedrooms available. If you want to splurge, request one of the two in front with a romantic balcony overlooking the lake. The moderately sized, spotlessly clean guestrooms are simple and attractive, with built-in wooden furniture and matching drapes and bedspreads. Each has a modern bathroom, air conditioning, telephone, TV, and mini bar. As in so many of our favorite hotels, the gracious owners, Jeannine and Jean-François Kung, are also the managers, always keeping an eye out to be sure the hotel is impeccable in every way. *Directions:* Yvoire is on the south shore of Lake Geneva, 30 km east of Geneva.

HÔTEL DU PORT
Hosts: Jeannine & Jean-François Kung
74140 Yvoire, France
Tel: 04.50.72.80.17, Fax: 04.50.72.90.71
4 rooms, Double: 640F–890F
No table d'hôte, restaurant
Open mid-Mar to Nov, Credit cards: all major
Very good English spoken
Region: Haute-Savoie, Michelin Map 244

Beynac, Dordogne

Key and Regional Map

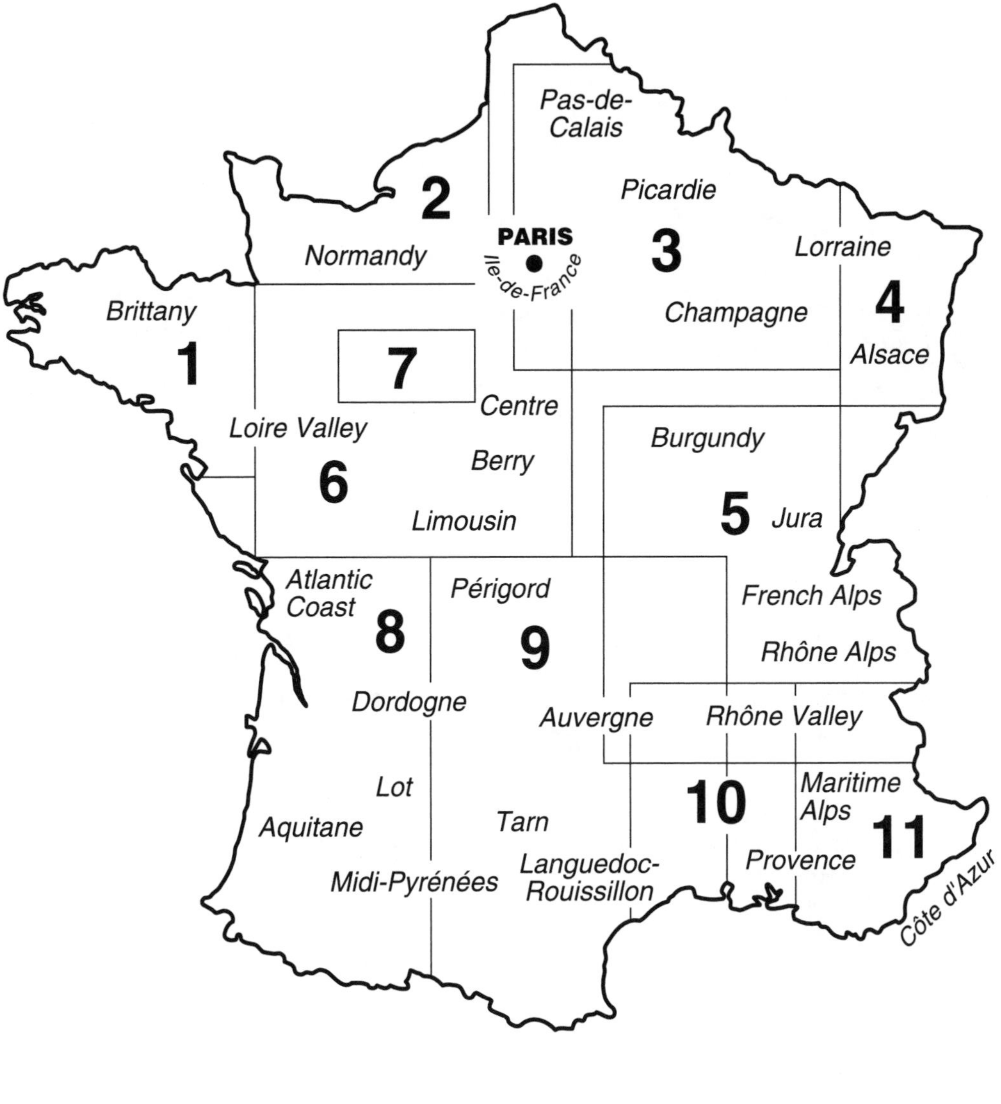

Pas-de-Calais

Picardie

2

Normandy

PARIS
Ile-de-France

3

Lorraine

4

Champagne

Alsace

Brittany

1

7

Centre

Burgundy

Loire Valley

Berry

6

5

Jura

Limousin

Atlantic Coast

Périgord

French Alps

8

9

Rhône Alps

Dordogne

Auvergne

Rhône Valley

Lot

Maritime Alps

10

11

Aquitane

Tarn

Provence

Midi-Pyrénées

Languedoc-Rouissillon

Côte d'Azur

Map 1

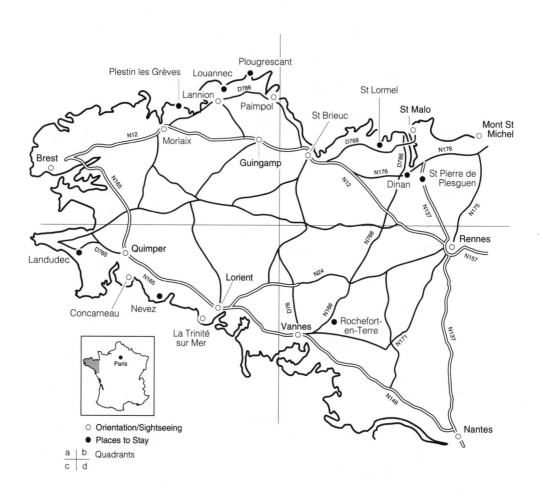

Plougrescant

Plestin les Grèves   Louannec

Lannion   D786

Paimpol

St Lormel

St Brieuc

St Malo

Mont St
Michel

N12   Morlaix

Brest   Guingamp   D768

N176

N165   N12   N176   D786

Dinan   St Pierre de
Plesguen

N137   N175

Quimper   N766   Rennes

Landudec   D765   N157

Lorient   N24

Concarneau   N165   Nevez   D76   N166

La Trinité   Vannes   Rochefort-
sur Mer   en-Terre

N171   N137

N149

Nantes

Paris

○ Orientation/Sightseeing
● Places to Stay

a	b
c	d

Quadrants

Map 2

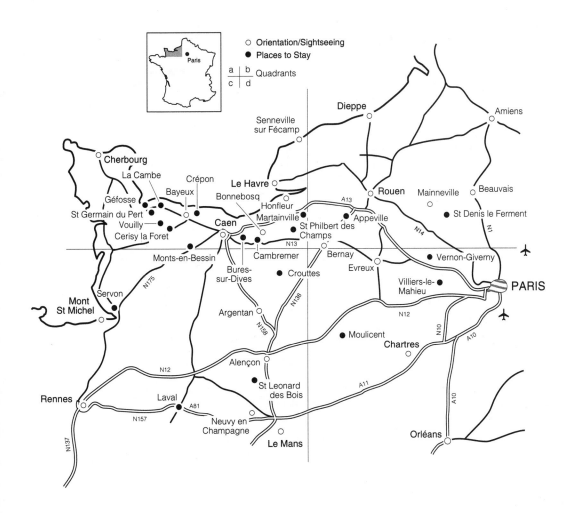

Orientation/Sightseeing
Places to Stay

a | b
c | d
Quadrants

Paris

Dieppe
Amiens
Senneville
sur Fécamp
Cherbourg
La Cambe
Crépon
Le Havre
Rouen
Mainneville
Beauvais
Bayeux
Bonnebosq
Géfosse
Honfleur
A13
St Germain du Pert
Martainville
Appeville
St Denis le Ferment
Caen
St Philbert des
Champs
N14
N1
Vouilly
Cerisy la Foret
N13
Monts-en-Bessin
Cambremer
Bernay
Vernon-Giverny
Bures-
sur-Dives
Croutres
Evreux
Villiers-le-
Mahieu
PARIS
Mont
St Michel
Servon
N175
Argentan
N138
N12
Moulicent
Chartres
N158
N10
A10
Alençon
N12
St Leonard
des Bois
A11
Rennes
Laval
A81
N157
Neuvy en
Champagne
N137
Le Mans
Orléans

Map 3

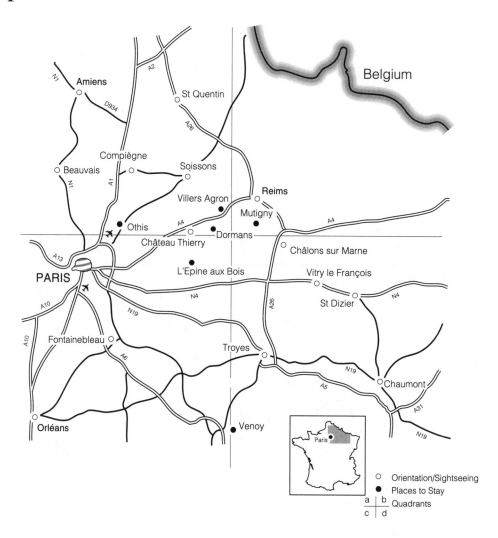

Map 4

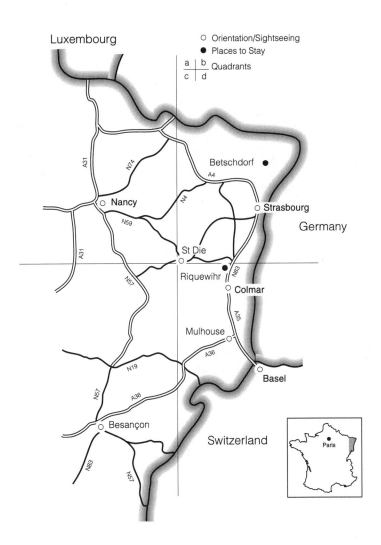

Luxembourg

○ Orientation/Sightseeing
● Places to Stay

a	b	Quadrants
c	d

A31

N74

Betschdorf ●

A4

Nancy ○

N4

N59

Strasbourg ○

Germany

A31

St Die ○

Riquewihr ●

N57

N83

Colmar ○

A35

Mulhouse ○

A36

N19

Basel ○

N57

A36

Besançon ○

Switzerland

N83

N57

Paris ●

Map 5

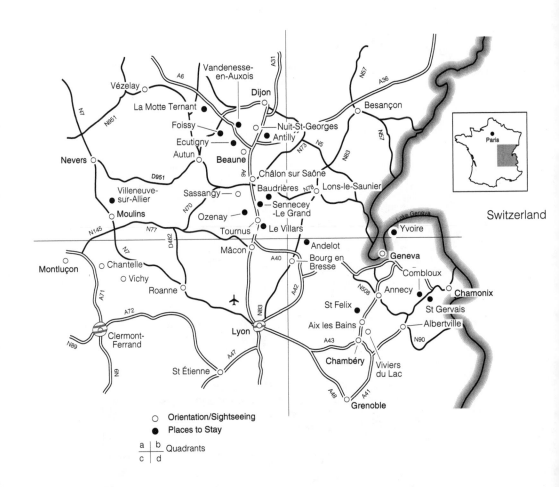

- ○ Orientation/Sightseeing
- ● Places to Stay

a	b
c	d

Quadrants

Map 6

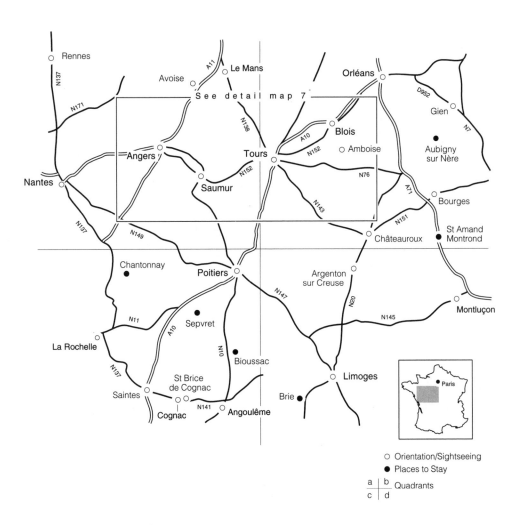

Rennes

N137

Avoise

Le Mans

A11

N171

Orléans

See detail map 7

D952

Gien

N138

A10 Blois

N7

N152

Amboise

Angers

Tours

Aubigny
sur Nère

N152

N76

A71

Nantes

Saumur

N143

Bourges

N137

N149

N151

St Amand
Montrond

Châteauroux

Chantonnay

Poitiers

Argenton
sur Creuse

N147

N20

N145

Montluçon

N11

A10

Sepvret

N10

La Rochelle

Bioussac

N137

St Brice
de Cognac

Limoges

Saintes

Brie

Cognac

N141

Angoulême

Paris

○ Orientation/Sightseeing
● Places to Stay

a	b
c	d

Quadrants

Map 7

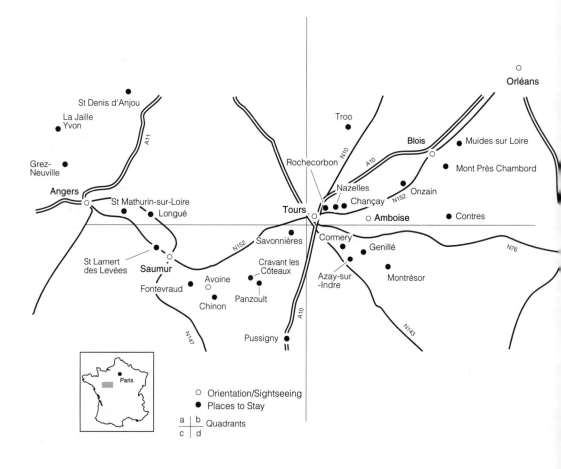

St Denis d'Anjou

La Jaille
Yvon

Grez-
Neuville

Angers

St Mathurin-sur-Loire

Longué

A11

St Lamert
des Levées

Saumur

Fontevraud

Avoine

Chinon

Panzoult

Cravant les
Côteaux

N147

N152

Savonnières

Pussigny

A10

Troo

Rochecorbon

N10

Tours

Nazelles

Chançay

Cormery

Azay-sur
-Indre

Genillé

Montrésor

N143

Blois

A10

Onzain

N152

Amboise

Mont Près Chambord

Muides sur Loire

Contres

N76

Orléans

Paris

○ Orientation/Sightseeing
● Places to Stay

a	b
c	d

Quadrants

Map 8

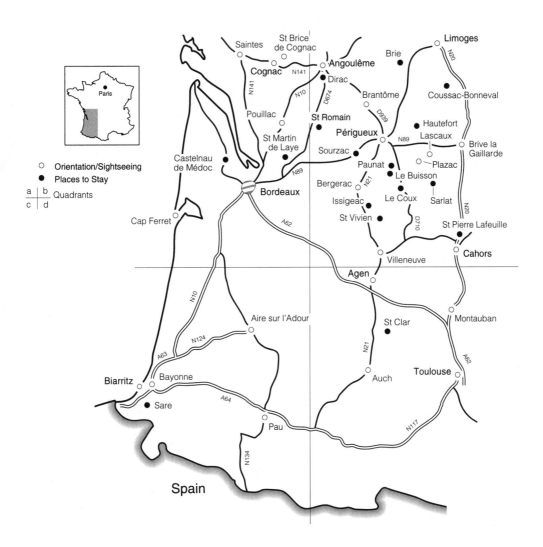

Saintes
St Brice de Cognac
Limoges
Brie
Cognac
N141
Angoulême
N141
N10
Dirac
Coussac-Bonneval
Pouillac
Brantôme
D939
St Romain
Hautefort
Lascaux
St Martin de Laye
Périgueux
N89
Brive la Gaillarde
Castelnau de Médoc
Sourzac
Plazac
Paunat
Le Buisson
Bordeaux
Bergerac
N21
Le Coux
Sarlat
Issigeac
N89
St Vivien
D710
St Pierre Lafeuille
Cap Ferret
A62
Villeneuve
Cahors
Agen
N10
N10
St Clar
Montauban
Aire sur l'Adour
N124
N21
A63
A62
Biarritz
Bayonne
Auch
Toulouse
A64
Sare
N117
Pau
N134
Spain

Paris

○ Orientation/Sightseeing
● Places to Stay

a	b
c	d

Quadrants

Map 9

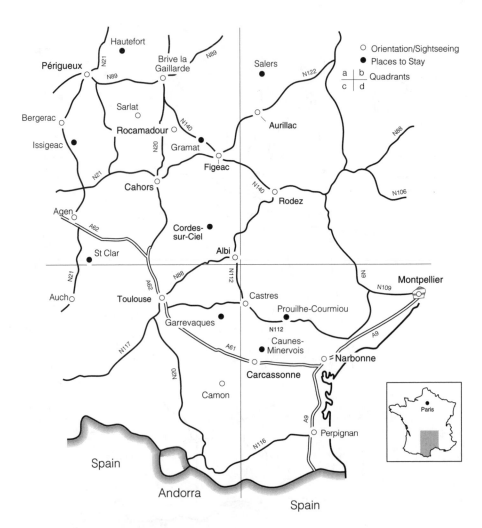

Hautefort

Brive la Gaillarde

Salers

N89

N122

○ Orientation/Sightseeing
● Places to Stay

a	b	Quadrants
c	d	

Périgueux

N21

N89

Bergerac

Sarlat

Issigeac

Rocamadour

N140

Aurillac

N88

Gramat

N20

Figeac

N140

Rodez

N106

Cahors

N21

Agen

Cordes-sur-Ciel

N88

Albi

A62

St Clar

Montpellier

N21

A62

N112

N9

Auch

Toulouse

Castres

N109

Garrevaques

Prouilhe-Courmiou

A9

N112

N117

Caunes-Minervois

A61

Narbonne

N20

Carcassonne

Camon

Spain

A9

Perpignan

Paris

Andorra

N116

Spain

Map 10

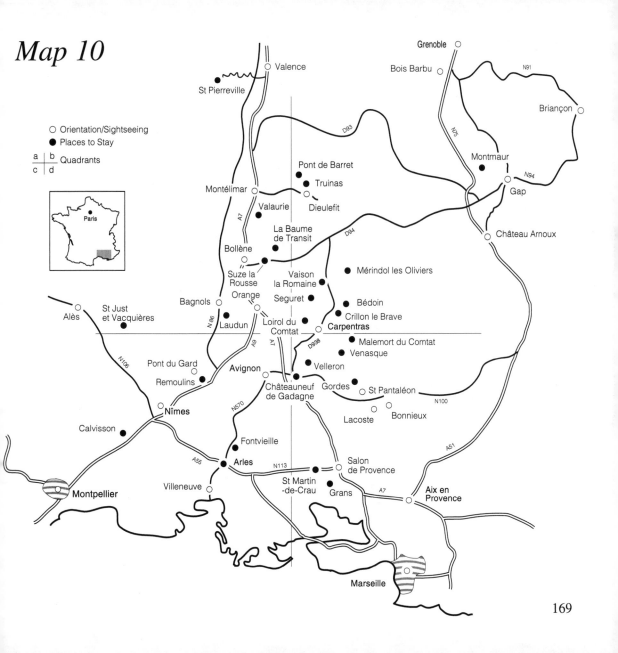

Grenoble

Bois Barbu

N91

Briançon

Valence

St Pierreville

○ Orientation/Sightseeing
● Places to Stay

a	b
c	d

Quadrants

Paris

Montmaur

N75

N94

Gap

Pont de Barret

Truinas

Montélimar

Valaurie

Dieulefit

A7

La Baume
de Transit

D94

Château Arnoux

Bollène

Suze la
Rousse

Vaison
la Romaine

Mérindol les Oliviers

St Just
et Vacquières

Bagnols

Orange

Seguret

Bédoin

Alès

N 86

Laudun

Loirol du
Comtat

Crillon le Brave

Carpentras

N106

Pont du Gard

A9

A7

D938

Malemort du Comtat

Venasque

Avignon

Velleron

Remoulins

Châteauneuf
de Gadagne

Gordes

St Pantaléon

N100

Nîmes

N570

Lacoste

Bonnieux

Calvisson

Fontvieille

A55

Arles

N113

Salon
de Provence

Villeneuve

St Martin
-de-Crau

Grans

A7

Aix en
Provence

Montpellier

A51

Marseille

169

Map 11

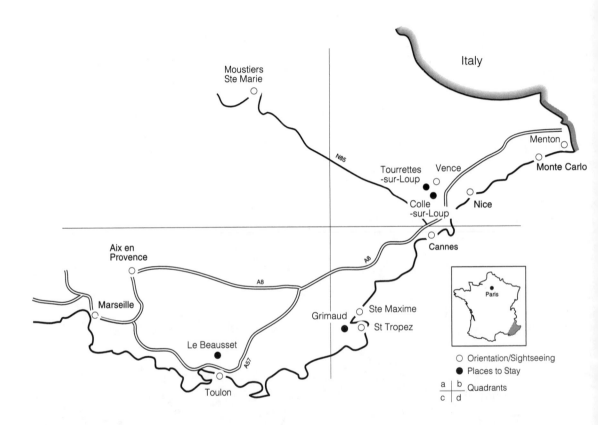

Italy

Moustiers
Ste Marie ○

N85

Tourrettes
-sur-Loup ●   Vence ○

Colle
-sur-Loup ●

Menton ○

Monte Carlo ●

Nice ○

Cannes ○

Aix en
Provence ○

A8

A8

Marseille ○

Grimaud ●   ○ Ste Maxime

○ St Tropez

Le Beausset ●

A57

Toulon ○

Paris ●

○ Orientation/Sightseeing
● Places to Stay

a	b	Quadrants
c	d

Index

SHARE YOUR DISCOVERIES WITH US

Outstanding properties often come from readers' discoveries. We would love to hear from you.

Please list below any hotel or bed & breakfast you discover. Tell us what you liked about the property and, if possible, please include a brochure or photographs so we can share your enthusiasm. We keep a permanent database of all of your recommendations for future use. Note: we regret we cannot return photos.

Owner _____ Hotel or B&B _____ Street _____

Town _____ Zip _____ State or Region _____ Country _____

Comments:

Your name _____ Street _____ Town _____ State _____

Zip _____ Country _____ Tel _____ e-mail _____ date _____

Would you be willing to share your discovery with other Karen Brown readers?

Do we have your permission to electronically publish your review(s) on our website? Yes _____ No _____

If yes, would you like commentary annonymous, Yes ___No ___, or may we use your name? Yes___ No___

Please send report to: Karen Brown's Guides, Post Office Box 70, San Mateo, California 94401, USA
tel: (650) 342-9117, fax: (650) 342-9153, e-mail: karen@karenbrown.com, www.karenbrown.com

CRITIQUE PLACES IN OUR BOOK

We greatly appreciate first-hand evaluations of places in our guides. Your critiques are invaluable to us. To stay current on the properties in our guides, we keep a database of readers' comments. To keep our readers up to date, we also sometimes share feedback with them via our website.

Please list your comments on properties that you have visited. We welcome accolades, as well as criticisms.

Name of hotel or b&b _____ Town _____ Country _____

Comments:

Name of hotel or b&b _____ Town _____ Country _____

Comments:

Your name _____ Street _____ Town _____ State _____

Zip _____ Country _____ Tel _____ e-mail _____ date _____

Do we have your permission to electronically publish your comments on our website? Yes _____ No _____

If yes, would you like commentary anonymous, Yes ___No ___, or may we use your name? Yes___ No___

Please send report to: Karen Brown's Guides, Post Office Box 70, San Mateo, California 94401, USA
tel: (650) 342-9117, fax: (650) 342-9153, e-mail: karen@karenbrown.com, www.karenbrown.com

Enhance Your Guides

Travel Your Dreams
Online

www.karenbrown.com

- Hotel News
- Color Photos
- New Discoveries
- Corrections & Edits
- Leisure Destinations
- Property of the Month
- Postcards from the Road
- Romantic Inns & Recipes

KB Travel Service

❖ **KB Travel Service** offers travel planning assistance using itineraries designed by *Karen Brown* and published in her guidebooks. We will customize any itinerary to fit your personal interests.

❖ We will plan your itinerary with you, help you decide how long to stay and what to do once you arrive, and work out the details.

❖ We will book your airline tickets and your rental car, arrange rail tickets or passes (including your seat reservations), reserve accommodations recommended in *Karen Brown's Guides,* and supply you with point-to-point information and consultation.

Contact us to start planning your travel!

800 782-2128 ext. 328 or e-mail: info@kbtravelservice.com

Service fees do apply

KB Travel Service

16 East Third Avenue
San Mateo, CA 94401 USA
www.kbtravelservice.com

Independently owned and operated by Town & Country Travel
CST 2001543-10

is the

Preferred Airline

of

Karen Brown's Guides

auto ⊕ europe.

Karen Brown's

Preferred Car Rental Service Provider

for

Worldwide Car Rental Services
Chauffeur & Transfer Services
Prestige & Sports Cars
Motor Home Rentals

1-800-223-5555

Be sure to identify yourself as a Karen Brown Traveler.
For special offers and discounts use your
Karen Brown ID number 99006187.

Become a Karen Brown Preferred Reader

Name _____

Street _____

Town _____

State _____ Zip _____ Country _____

Tel _____ Fax _____

E-mail _____

We'd love to welcome you as a Karen Brown Preferred Reader. Send us your name and address and you will be entered in our monthly drawing to receive a free set of Karen Brown guides. As a preferred reader, you will receive special promotions and be the first to know when new editions of Karen Brown guides go to press.

Please send to: Karen Brown's Guides, Post Office Box 70, San Mateo, California 94401, USA
tel: (650) 342-9117, fax: (650) 342-9153, e-mail: karen@karenbrown.com, website: www: karenbrown.com

Notes

Seal Cove Inn

Located in the San Francisco Bay Area

Karen Brown Herbert (best known as author of the Karen Brown's guides) and her husband, Rick, have put 22 years of experience into reality and opened their own superb hideaway, Seal Cove Inn. Spectacularly set amongst wild flowers and bordered by towering cypress trees, Seal Cove Inn looks out to the distant ocean over acres of county park: an oasis where you can enjoy secluded beaches, explore tidepools, watch frolicking seals, and follow the tree-lined path that traces the windswept ocean bluffs. Country antiques, original watercolors, flower-laden cradles, rich fabrics, and the gentle ticking of grandfather clocks create the perfect ambiance for a foggy day in front of the crackling log fire. Each bedroom is its own haven with a cozy sitting area before a wood-burning fireplace and doors opening onto a private balcony or patio with views to the park and ocean. Moss Beach is a 35-minute drive south of San Francisco, 6 miles north of the picturesque town of Half Moon Bay, and a few minutes from Princeton harbor with its colorful fishing boats and restaurants. Seal Cove Inn makes a perfect base for whale-watching, salmon-fishing excursions, day trips to San Francisco, exploring the coast, or, best of all, just a romantic interlude by the sea, time to relax and be pampered. Karen and Rick look forward to the pleasure of welcoming you to their coastal hideaway.

Seal Cove Inn • 221 Cypress Avenue • Moss Beach • California • 94038 • USA
tel: (650) 728-4114, fax: (650) 728-4116, e-mail: sealcove@coastside.net, website: sealcoveinn.com

TRAVELSMITH®

Need a dual voltage hair dryer, a wrinkle-free blazer, quick-dry clothes, a computer adapter plug? TRAVELSMITH has them all, along with an enticing array of everything a Karen Brown traveler needs.

Karen Brown recommends TRAVELSMITH as an excellent source for travel clothing and gear. We were pleased to find quality products needed for our own research travels in their catalog—items not always easy to find. For a free catalog call TRAVELSMITH at 800-950-1600.

When placing your order, be sure to identify yourself as a Karen Brown Traveler with the code TKB99 and you will receive a 10% discount*. You can link to TRAVELSMITH through our website *www.karenbrown.com.*

*offer valid till December 2000

Travel Your Dreams • Order your Karen Brown Guides Today

Please ask in your local bookstore for Karen Brown's Guides. If the books you want are unavailable, you may order directly from the publisher. Books will be shipped immediately.

_____ *Austria: Charming Inns & Itineraries* $18.95

_____ *California: Charming Inns & Itineraries* $18.95

_____ *England: Charming Bed & Breakfasts* $17.95

_____ *England, Wales & Scotland: Charming Hotels & Itineraries* $18.95

_____ *France: Charming Bed & Breakfasts* $17.95

_____ *France: Charming Inns & Itineraries* $18.95

_____ *Germany: Charming Inns & Itineraries* $18.95

_____ *Ireland: Charming Inns & Itineraries* $18.95

_____ *Italy: Charming Bed & Breakfasts* $17.95

_____ *Italy: Charming Inns & Itineraries* $18.95

_____ *Portugal: Charming Inns & Itineraries* $18.95

_____ *Spain: Charming Inns & Itineraries* $18.95

_____ *Switzerland: Charming Inns & Itineraries* $18.95

Name _____ Street _____

Town _____ State _____ Zip _____ Tel _____

Credit Card (MasterCard or Visa) _____ Expires: _____

For orders in the USA, add $4 for the first book and $1 for each additional book for shipment. California residents add 8.25% sales tax. Overseas orders add $10 per book for airmail shipment. Indicate number of copies of each title; fax or mail form with check or credit card information to:

KAREN BROWN'S GUIDES
Post Office Box 70 • San Mateo • California • 94401 • USA
tel: (650) 342-9117, fax: (650) 342-9153, e-mail: karen@karenbrown.com
You can also order directly from our website at www.karenbrown.com.

KAREN BROWN wrote her first travel guide in 1976. Her personalized travel series has grown to thirteen titles which Karen and her small staff work diligently to keep updated. Karen, her husband, Rick, and their children, Alexandra and Richard, live in Moss Beach, a small town on the coast south of San Francisco. They settled here in 1991 when they opened Seal Cove Inn. Karen is frequently traveling, but when she is home, in her role as innkeeper, enjoys welcoming Karen Brown readers.

CLARE BROWN, CTC, was a travel consultant for many years, specializing in planning itineraries to Europe using charming small hotels in the countryside. The focus of her job remains unchanged, but now her expertise is available to a larger audience—the readers of her daughter Karen's country inn guides. When Clare and her husband, Bill, are not traveling, they live either in Hillsborough, California, or at their home in Vail, Colorado, where family and friends frequently join them for skiing.

JUNE BROWN'S love of travel was inspired by the *National Geographic* magazines that she read as a girl in her dentist's office—so far she has visited over 40 countries. June hails from Sheffield, England and lived in Zambia and Canada before moving to northern California where she lives in San Mateo with her husband, Tony, their daughter Clare, their German Shepherd, and a Siamese cat.

BARBARA TAPP, the talented artist who produces all of the hotel sketches and delightful illustrations in this guide, was raised in Australia where she studied in Sydney at the School of Interior Design. Although Barbara continues with freelance projects, she devotes much of her time to illustrating the Karen Brown guides. Barbara lives in Kensington, California, with her husband, Richard, their two sons, Jonothan and Alexander, and daughter, Georgia.

JANN POLLARD, the artist responsible for the beautiful painting on the cover of this guide, has studied art since childhood, and is well-known for her outstanding impressionistic-style watercolors which she has exhibited in numerous juried shows, winning many awards. Jann travels frequently to Europe (using Karen Brown's guides) where she loves to paint historical buildings. Jann lives in Burlingame, California, with her husband, Gene.